M000195644

The Innocents

A New Play

by William Archibald

Based on *The Turn of the Screw*
by Henry James

A Samuel French Acting Edition

SAMUEL
FRENCH

FOUNDED 1830

New York   Hollywood   London   Toronto

SAMUELFRENCH.COM

THE INNOCENTS

STORY OF THE PLAY

The Innocents is connected with a sensitive young governess who assumes the guidance of two highly imaginative and precocious youngsters, orphans, at an English country house in 1880. Due to the negligence of a self-centered uncle, they have been subjected to the bad influence of a couple of seamy servants.

Though both of these have died, their evil examples survive. They reappear as ghosts, but when you have left the theatre there is still the question of whether they were literal ghosts or figments of the mind. That you will have to determine for yourself.

The governess sends the girl away to safety, and remains behind with the boy to dispel, once and for all, the delusions and the memories that have corrupted him. And that is a scene to make you sit forward on the edge of your seat.

THE INNOCENTS

Play by William Archibald; adapted from Henry James' story "The Turn of the Screw"; staged by Peter Glenville; scenery by Jo Mielziner; costumes by Motley; music by Alex North; presented by Peter Cookson at the Playhouse Theatre, February 1, 1950. The cast:

FLORA .... *Iris Mann*
MRS. GROSE .... *Isobel Elsom*
MISS GIDDENS ... *Beatrice Straight*
MILES .... *David Cole*

Also: *Andrew Duggan and Ella Playwin.*

SYNOPSIS: *The drawing-room of a country house in England, 1880.*

ACT ONE

SCENE 1: *An early autumn afternoon.*
SCENE 2: *Three hours later.*
SCENE 3: *The following morning.*
SCENE 4: *Twilight. The same day.*
SCENE 5. *The following morring.*

ACT TWO

SCENE 1: *Evening of the same day.*
SCENE 2: *The next morning.*
SCENE 3: *The same day. Twilight.*

4

The Innocents

ACT ONE

SCENE I

House light to half: Warn MUSIC A.
House light out Go MUSIC A (Volume 45).
"Bright Rosy Red" (Orchestra); Curtain up.
*   Volume to 15.*
Second "Roses On It": Volume to 10.
MUSIC end: LIGHTS up.

SCENE: *The drawing-room of an old country house in Essex, England.*

The room is large, high-ceilinged. Directly Center of rear wall, a French window opens onto a garden. It is a window that rises up and up until its summit is half-lost in the shadows of the ceiling; heavy, dark curtains hang framing it—these can be drawn by pulling at the cord that hangs to Right of window. Lighter silk curtains hang across window —these, too, can be drawn together.

To the Left of Center is a plush-covered love-seat; back of love-seat is a graceful desk on which are accessories for letterwriting and a lamp. Back of desk is a chair; a table Right of desk; an otto-man at Center; and armchair Right; a spinet and stool up Right; a cabinet in alcove up Left. There is a door down Right and another up Left.

A staircase rises from down Right, to up Right. On landing at head of staircase is an unseen door to two rooms; beside this door stands a grandfather clock. From the landing, a passage is suggested, leading off, Right. Above landing, Right, and unseen, is a small skylight which, depending on the time of day, allows some light to fall onto top chair.

(This setting, the only one used throughout, should be secondary to the light within it. The walls should be free of decoration, and of shades of one color. All exits should be undecorated and of the same color as the walls, so that they are not apparent until opened. The French window should seem to be the only entrance and exit to the room. A carpet, of a color that supports that of the walls, covers the entire floor space and the stairs and landing.)

TIME: *About 1860.*

AT RISE: *At rise of Curtain, the curtains at the French window are open.*

It is four-thirty o'clock in the afternoon. Sunlight floods the room.

FLORA *sits at the spinet. She is a little girl, eight years old, with long hair tied with a neat bow. She sits with straight back, her feet barely touching the floor.*

(As Curtain rises, the orchestral variation of "O Bring Me A Bonnet" gives way to sound of the piano.)

FLORA. *(Singing as she plays the piano)*

    O bring me a bonnet,
    O bring me a bonnet,
    O bring me a bonnet of bright rosy red—
    With white roses on it,
    With white roses on it,
    O bring me a bonnet to wear on my head—

(The melody seems to be repeated far away. FLORA turns quickly as MRS. GROSE enters from door down Right. MRS. GROSE is in her sixties and wears the starched apron and frilly cap of a housekeeper of the period.)

MRS. GROSE. Have you been sitting quietly, Miss Flora?

FLORA. I haven't been doing anything else for hours. Where have you been, Mrs. Grose?

MRS. GROSE. *(An excitement apparent in her every movement)* You've rumpled your dress— Now, Miss Flora—

FLORA. *(Smiling, teasing as MRS. GROSE pulls at her sash)* O, no! That's a tuck that was always there—

MRS. GROSE. It wasn't this morning. Now, do sit down and don't muss yourself.

FLORA. There'd be less chance of that if I remain standing, don't you think? When will she get here, Mrs. Grose?

MRS. GROSE. *(Dusting things already spotless)* At any moment—the carriage'll bring her soon— Did *you* put those leaves in her room?

FLORA. They are pretty, aren't they?

MRS. GROSE. Leaves! With a whole garden of flowers!

FLORA. *(Following MRS. GROSE about the room)* Is my uncle coming with her?

MRS. GROSE. *(Paying little attention to her)* Your uncle?

FLORA. I expect he's too busy— *(Pause)* Is she very pretty?

MRS. GROSE. *(Preoccupied)* I'm sure she is.

FLORA. She might be ugly. Do I need another governess?

MRS. GROSE. Why, yes. You'll like her—won't you?

FLORA. O, yes— Will Miles like her?

MRS. GROSE. Master Miles? Of course.

FLORA. He'll be home from school soon—

MRS. GROSE. For the holidays. Not before.

FLORA. He might be. Mightn't he, Mrs. Grose? Before that?

MRS. GROSE. There'd be no reason. *(Turns—her face puckering up)* O, Miss Flora, lamb! You miss him, don't you?

FLORA. I'm not lonely—though I'd like to see Miles. I'd like it if he were *always* here.

MRS. GROSE. Of course you would, precious. But Miss Giddens will think of things to do—and won't she be amazed at how clever you are—!

FLORA. Am I? *(As MRS. GROSE nods)* Then—do I need another governess? And—are all governess' alike?

MRS. GROSE. *(Continuing to dust and rearrange furniture)* They're different as one person is from another.

FLORA. *(Thoughtfully)* It'd be an interesting thing if she'd let me get all dirty then put me to bed without a bath—

MRS. GROSE. *(Hardly listening as she dusts)* Ha!

FLORA. Perhaps I won't have to study my books—perhaps we'll spend the time with conversations or, if we feel like it on a particular day, we might just sit and stare at each other—lots of people do—

MRS. GROSE. Only when they have nothing to say. There's no chance of *that* with *you* around.

FLORA. When I don't talk you think I'm ill—

MRS. GROSE. Ha! Is that why you have so much to say? *(Fondly)* I don't believe it!

FLORA. Things pop into my head. There doesn't seem much sense in leaving them there—

MRS. GROSE. *(Paying little attention to her)* Don't you get all hot and mussy, now, Miss Flora.

FLORA. How could I? I'm standing still—and, do you know? *(Looks slowly up at the ceiling)* I feel quite small when I'm not moving—

MRS. GROSE. You'll grow soon enough.

FLORA. O, it's not *that*, Mrs. Grose? Why do people run past tall trees?

MRS. GROSE. I haven't got time for riddles, Miss Flora.

FLORA. It isn't a *riddle.* *(Wandering over to the window)* I feel terribly small— I feel as though I could crawl under the carpet and be completely flat—

(LIGHT #1. Stairway dim.)

MRS. GROSE. If you go on feeling you'll make yourself ill.

FLORA. *(Singing)* "O, Bring Me A Bonnet." *(Looking out to garden)* O, it's lovely watching a person come at you from a long way off!

MRS. GROSE. You'll be sick.

FLORA. *(Still looking out)* Of course she may not like it here. Then she'll pack her things and leave—

MRS. GROSE. *(On her knees—peering under spinet)* Do you put leaves under here just to tease me, Miss Flora? If you must bring leaves into the house, couldn't you put them in a box?

FLORA. *(Not turning)* They'd stifle. She's coming up the drive—and she isn't in a carriage at all— *(Turns from the window—wide-eyed)* She's walking—

MRS. GROSE. *(All nervous excitement, now, crumbling the leaves in her hand, letting them drop as she gets to her feet)* Is it Miss Giddens, Miss Flora? Or are you teasing? And why would she be walking? The carriage went to fetch her— *(Bending down to pick up leaves.)*

FLORA. She has just a *little* bag in her hand—wouldn't she have a trunk if she's going to stay?

MRS. GROSE. O, dear! She couldn't carry her trunk— Everything was so neat— What will she think?

FLORA. There, there. Everything is neat. I'll close the piano—then *everything* will be tidy. *(Closes the spinet with all the seriousness of a well behaved child)* Now. Shall I go to the window and go to meet her?

MRS. GROSE. No, no. It's not in your place as a little lady. Sit quietly, Miss Flora— *(She pushes the window open, then waits on the threshold, patting at the creases in her apron, straightening her cap, looking off to Left.*

As MRS. GROSE *opens window,* FLORA *sits on love-seat. To the person who comes walking up the drive)* Miss Giddens?

(FLORA *turns her head to French window.)*

MISS GIDDENS. *(From garden. Her voice is youthful and breathless)* It's beautiful! It's all so beautiful! The gardens, I mean— I had to walk from the gate— I had to see it all! The carriage took my trunk around to the back— I hope you don't mind?

MRS. GROSE. *(Stepping backwards into the room)* Dear, no— I thought the carriage had missed you— *(Turning)* Miss Flora—here is Miss Giddens—

(MISS GIDDENS *steps into the room. She is young, pretty, dressed for travelling. She carries a small bag.)*

MISS GIDDENS. *(As* FLORA *curtsies to her)* How do you do, Flora? (FLORA *curtsies again, smiling.)* And you—you are Mrs. Grose—the housekeeper, of course?

MRS. GROSE. *(Curtseying)* Yes, Miss—and you must forgive me. I meant to have tea ready for you—but, now—I'll have it here if you don't mind waiting a moment— *(She goes, in confusion, to door Right, then turns, flushed and beaming)* I'm *glad* you've come— *(Exits.)*

MISS GIDDENS. *(To* MRS. GROSE) Thank you. Well, Flora—?

(MISS GIDDENS *and* FLORA *stand, silently for a moment, smiling at each other.)*

FLORA. Would you like to take off your hat?

MISS GIDDENS. *(Sitting on love-seat, taking off hat)* Thank you—

FLORA. *(Taking hat from her)* I shall put it here— Won't you sit down? *(Puts it on desk.)*

MISS GIDDENS. Thank you. Come sit by me— (FLORA

goes to sit on love-seat.) We must get to know each other, you know—

FLORA. O, I'm sure we will. You're staying, aren't you? You told Mrs. Grose your trunk was here—

MISS GIDDENS. *(Laughing)* Why, of course I'm staying! I wouldn't be much of a governess if I didn't— now would I? So, I *shall— (Wooing her)* —if you'd like me to?

FLORA. O, yes— *(Pauses)* I hope you'll like your room—

MISS GIDDENS. I'm sure it's lovely—

FLORA. If you don't—you may choose another— There are thirty-five—most of them closed—and think of it! One hundred and forty windows! Shall we go into the garden and count them?

MISS GIDDENS. *(Charmed by the politeness)* I *would* like to—but poor Mrs. Grose would be alone with her tea—and I did say I'd like some.

FLORA. *You* didn't. *She* said she'd get it.

MISS GIDDENS. *(Taken aback—laughing)* O— It wouldn't be polite, now would it? To go walking in the garden?

FLORA. *I* often do. There are several ways you can walk, you know, if you don't walk on the drive—

MISS GIDDENS. *(Nonplussed—but trying)* Several ways? You mean hopping and skipping?

FLORA. *(In amazement)* Do *you* hop and skip?

MISS GIDDENS. I do—on occasion—

FLORA. I've never had a governess who did *that*—

MISS GIDDENS. Well, we're each a little different.

FLORA. (FLORA's *smile disappears)* "Different"?

MISS GIDDENS. (MISS GIDDENS, *puzzled, laughs after a pause that, because of its suddenness, seems much longer than it actually is)* Just as you are different from —from, well say: Mrs. Grose— (FLORA *does not move, nor does she seem to be listening.* MISS GIDDENS *makes another try)* You're eight years old, aren't you, dear?

(CHIMES.)

FLORA. Yes—

MISS GIDDENS. And Miles? He's twelve, isn't he?

FLORA. Yes—

MISS GIDDENS. And as good as you are, I'm sure!

FLORA. *(In a very small voice)* I expect we're both a little naughty sometimes—

MISS GIDDENS. *(Drawing FLORA to her, kissing her on her cheek)* Of course you are! And I shall love you for it!

MRS. GROSE. *(Entering from Right, carrying a tray of tea things)* You're famished for a cup, I'm sure—after your long journey—so I'll set it down and leave you and the little lady to talk— *(Sets tray on desk—turns to Right.)*

MISS GIDDENS. Mrs. Grose? Won't you sit with me a while? There're things I'd like to ask you—

MRS. GROSE. Things, Miss?

MISS GIDDENS. Yes— I don't know the habits of the house—it would make it easier if you told me—

MRS. GROSE. Why, yes, if you'd like, Miss. *(Remains standing, Right of desk.)*

MISS GIDDENS. *(Rising)* Will you have some tea, Flora?

FLORA. No, thank you.

MISS GIDDENS. *(Going to desk)* Do sit down, Mrs. Grose.

MRS. GROSE. *(Sitting on chair at desk)* Thank you, Miss—

MISS GIDDENS. (MISS GIDDENS *pours tea into cups—as she does this she starts to laugh softly, looking at* MRS. GROSE, *then* FLORA, *who sits quietly)* And I was so afraid!

FLORA. *(Wonderingly)* Afraid?

MISS GIDDENS. Timid, Flora—couldn't make up my mind for days— Should I accept this post—should I? Shouldn't I? None of my brothers or sisters could help me! I wouldn't ask advice! *(Laughs.)*

FLORA. *(Laughing)* I never take advice!

MRS. GROSE. *(Seriously)* Now, Miss Flora—

MISS GIDDENS. *(As she takes a cup of tea to* MRS.

GROSE, *who rises embarrassedly)* But why should one take advice, Mrs. Grose? Or give it? *(As* MRS. GROSE *remains standing—cup in hand—slightly ill-at-ease)* Do sit down, Mrs. Grose— *(As she returns to love-seat, sits)* Of course, advice is forced upon you, in as large a family as mine was—

FLORA. *(Fascinated)* How large?

MISS GIDDENS. Very large. In a very small house. Secrets were difficult.

FLORA. But "possible"?

MISS GIDDENS. Not for long.

FLORA. That *must* have been annoying.

MISS GIDDENS. Well— *(Laughing)* Of course we shared our secrets when we were your age—but grown-ups never knew—

FLORA. *(Laughing with her)* They never do—do they?

MRS. GROSE. Now, Miss Flora—

MISS GIDDENS. *(To* MRS. GROSE, *smiling)* Oh, they found out after awhile! My family believed in open doors and after-dinner conferences—

MRS. GROSE. And a very *sensible* thing, too, Miss—

FLORA. *(To* MISS GIDDENS) Is it?

MRS. GROSE. *(Vexedly)* Miss *Flora—*

MISS GIDDENS. *(Realizing that perhaps she has been a little too free with* FLORA) Yes, Flora. A *very* sensible thing— *(Smiling)* Now, wouldn't you like to walk in the garden while I speak to Mrs. Grose? *(She goes with* FLORA *to window.)*

FLORA. *(The perfect "obedient" child)* Why, yes, if you'd like me to, Miss Giddens.

MISS GIDDENS. And I'll come out when I've had a cup of tea— (FLORA *curtsies to her, goes through French window and out into garden.)* Poor little thing. She looks so lonely out there—

MRS. GROSE. Lonely, Miss? Most independent. Just as soon wander off by herself—though as easy with company as any—

MISS GIDDENS. *(Looking out)* She *is* lonely, though.

Perhaps it's because I grew up in a large family— Well, at least she has a beautiful garden to walk in— *(Softly)* It *is* a beautiful garden—so quiet, so peaceful— The thickness of the trees seem to form a wall between one path and another. As I walked under them I had a feeling of solitude—and yet, I also felt that I was not completely alone— *(Turning to* Mrs. Grose*)* When you walked in the garden—your first day here—what did you think, Mrs. Grose?

Mrs. Grose. *(Softly)* I was young, Miss— I thought it was all very beautiful—

Miss Giddens. *(Moving away from window; looking about room, taking in each detail of it)* How awful if it were an ugly one! *(She laughs softly)* How awful if this room were cold and ugly! I was almost afraid it might be! *(Returns to love-seat. Sits down; takes her cup.)*

Mrs. Grose. *(Puzzled)* Might be, Miss?

Miss Giddens. *(Seriously)* No. I didn't think that. I suppose I knew it would be beautiful—because his house on Harley Street was— *(Pause)* Mrs. Grose—perhaps it isn't any of my business—but he, their uncle, when I spoke to him—when he engaged me—he was so brief with me. He said he didn't want to be bothered by letters from me about the children— He said that, you know—he made it seem *the* important part of his terms. He said—under no condition was I to *bother him*. Doesn't he love them?

Mrs. Grose. *(Uncomfortably)* I'm sure he does—in his fashion, Miss, if you'll excuse me—

Miss Giddens. I don't understand how he could choose to ignore them. But I know so little— Only that their parents died soon after Miss Flora's birth and that *he* is their sole guardian—

Mrs. Grose. Yes, Miss— But you must understand, Miss— He's not a young man and he's never enjoyed good health— He was always a studious man—wrapped up in his work— He's never had any family responsibilities before— *(Gently)* But he does keep this house

on—especially for them. He *is* dong all that can be expected—

MISS GIDDENS. Yes, after all, Miles and Flora aren't
his children— And, he certainly *was* absorbed in his
work— He could scarcely spare the time to interview
me and spent most of it talking about his collection of
Chinese paintings— *(Looks about the room)* I see he's
got some of them here— I must admit they're rather
beautiful—but I couldn't help being angry when he
spoke to me about not bothering him about the children.
(Gently) You see, I have been in the midst of my family, first as a child, then as a guardian to my younger
brothers and sisters— *(Rising, moving about the room,
taking in the details of it)* It isn't enough to give a child
a house and garden as beautiful as these— *(Wryly)* I'm
afraid I showed him how angry I was. I'm afraid *that*
is why he engaged me—because I "stood up" to him. I
was caught. I showed how much I loved children—and
that I would do *anything* to make them happy. That was
all he wanted, apparently— Someone to take the responsibility off *his* shoulders. Well, here I am. *(Gently)*
And I'm embarrassing you— I don't mean to. *(Laughs)*
And what an easy task it will be! An affectionate task!
And all within a large roomy house surrounded by a
lovely garden! *(Determinedly)* And—when he pays us
a visit—

MRS. GROSE. I don't expect he will, Miss. He's been
here only once or twice that I can bring to mind. Though
there were times in the months just passed when—

MISS GIDDENS. *(Taken aback)* When *what*, Mrs.
Grose?

MRS. GROSE. When *he* should have been the one to
shoulder the—

MISS GIDDENS. The what, Mrs. Grose?

MRS. GROSE. Bygones is bygones.

MISS GIDDENS. Not if I'm to do my work satis-
factorily—

MRS. GROSE. Pardon me, Miss. It isn't to do with

you—you'd best forget I spoke—so—so out of place. *(She rises.)*

MISS GIDDENS. *(Stubbornly)* Mrs. Grose. What was she like?

MRS. GROSE. *(Uncomfortably)* Who, Miss?

MISS GIDDENS. The lady who was here before.

MRS. GROSE. The last governess? She was also young and pretty, Miss, even as you—

MISS GIDDENS. *(Smiling with embarrassment)* He doesn't mind them being young and pretty!

MRS. GROSE. *(Turning to her—vehemently)* Oh, no —it was the way he liked everyone! *(Flushing)* I mean —why should the Master mind?

MISS GIDDENS. But of whom did you speak *first?*

MRS. GROSE. *(Blankly)* Why, of *him.*

MISS GIDDENS. Of the Master? *(WARN Dimout.)*

MRS. GROSE. Of who else?

(They search each other's faces.)

MISS GIDDENS. *(Casually)* Mrs. Grose—was she— my predecessor—careful, particular—in her work?

MRS. GROSE. *(Against her will)* About some things —yes—

MISS GIDDENS. But not about all?

MRS. GROSE. Well, Miss, she's passed on. I won't tell tales.

MISS GIDDENS. *(Quickly)* I understand your feeling —but— Did she die here?

MRS. GROSE. No—she went away.

(FLORA appears at window.)

MISS GIDDENS. Went *away?* To die? She was taken ill you mean—and went home?

MRS. GROSE. She was not taken ill so far as *appeared* in this house. She—she left it to go home, she said, for a short holiday. At the very moment I was expecting her back I heard from the Master that she was dead.

Miss Giddens. But of what?

(The Two Women *stare at each other. Through scene, LIGHTS dim. Only from the French window comes a last ray of sunlight.)*

Flora. *(In a small, clear voice)* Miss Giddens— aren't you coming for a walk?

> *(LIGHTS. Count 2. MUSIC. A1, volume 8. Curtain. Vol. 45.)*

SLOW DIM

ACT ONE

Scene II

(Curtain up. MUSIC volume 8.)

Scene: *Three hours later.*
> *This scene begins in semi-darkness.* Miss Gidden's *voice overlaps transition music.*
> *LIGHTS come up slowly. A pale moonlight comes through the French window.*
> Miss Giddens *sits on the love-seat.* Flora *sits beside her, sleepily; she is wearing a long white nightgown.*
> *Candle, lighted, on desk.* Flora *leans against* Miss Giddens' *shoulder.*

Miss Giddens. *(Softly, reading from book)* "In the winter time, when deep snow lay on the ground, a poor boy was forced to go out on a sledge to fetch wood. When he had gathered it together, and packed it, he wished, as he was frozen with cold, not to go home at once but to light a fire and warm himself a little—"
Flora. How would he light it?

Miss Giddens. Well—I suppose he had a flint on which to strike—

Flora. Oh—

Miss Giddens. *(Reading)* "So—he scraped away the snow, and as he was thus cleaning the ground, he found —a tiny, golden key! Hereupon he thought that where the key was, the lock must be also—so he dug in the ground and found—an iron chest! 'If the key does but fit it!' thought he; 'no doubt there are precious things in that little box!' He searched, but no keyhole was there. At last—he discovered one! But so small that it was hardly visible. He tried it, and the key fitted it exactly. Then he turned it once round—and now we must wait until he has quite unlocked it and opened the lid— and then we shall learn what wonderful things were lying in that box."   *(MUSIC fades.)*

Flora. Was he a little boy like Miles?

Miss Giddens. He might even have *been* Miles.

Flora. Oh— What was in the box?

Miss Giddens. Why, we shall have to wait until it's opened.

Flora. *When* will it be?

Miss Giddens. It doesn't say—but it's fun guessing. What do *you* think is in the box?

Flora. I think I'd rather wait until it's opened—

Miss Giddens. And if it isn't?

Flora. Then I'll just *imagine* things.

Miss Giddens. *(More to herself than to* Flora*)* Yes— *(Closes book. Shivering as though a sudden draught has entered the room)* It's cold— Aren't you cold, dear?

Flora. No. *(Snuggling closer to* Miss Giddens*)* I'm half-asleep, I think. Shall I stay in your room tonight?

Miss Giddens. *(Looking about the room. Absentmindedly)* If you'd like to—   *(MUSIC B, volume 6.)*

Flora. Mrs. Grose wanted to give you a larger room —but I said: She'll only be there when she's asleep and big rooms have a way of growing bigger at night. Mrs.

Grose says they *don't*, but that's because *she* doesn't like the dark and won't open her eyes.

(MUSIC. Volume 15. Hold for 8 counts.)

(The SHADOW *of a man appears against the silk curtains of the window. As though a man had approached the window, the shadow looms until it fills the window.* FLORA *yawns, then she giggles.)*

FLORA. I wish there was some way to sleep in several rooms at once— Mrs. Grose was quite startled by the thought—

MISS GIDDENS. *(Laughing—a little nervously)* I don't wonder!

(The SHADOW *recedes as though the man steps away.)*

(MUSIC out.)

FLORA. *(Laughing)* She gets so upset about things like that! Do you know what she did about the rooms in the attic? *(*MISS GIDDENS *rises from the love-seat, a puzzled frown on her face. She looks toward window.)* Why—what's the matter, Miss Giddens, dear?

MISS GIDDENS. *(Smiling quickly)* Nothing. What about the attic rooms?

FLORA. They are empty, but you can see everything that once was in them!

MISS GIDDENS. *(Looking toward window again)* Can you—?

FLORA. Yes. The chairs—*everything*—has left a mark. It looks as though the pictures are still hanging and, if you look closely, you can see the carpet, though it's been rolled up and put away! *(She watches* MISS GIDDENS *and waits for a moment; then:)* Mrs. Grose doesn't like the idea. She has locked up all those rooms and several more— *(She yawns, watching* MISS GIDDENS, *who is looking about the room as though she senses something amiss)* But I— O, I wish my room was like that!

MISS GIDDENS. *(Looking at her—smiling—trying to appear unconcerned)* It'd—it'd be uncomfortable. Nothing to sit on—and how would you go to bed?

FLORA. I wouldn't. I'd much rather not, anyway.

MISS GIDDENS. *(Sitting down beside her again)* I'm afraid you'll have to—now.

FLORA. Must I? Then, first, tell me a story out of your head.

MISS GIDDENS. *(Once more preoccupied)* Out of my head?   *(Warn MUSIC C and dimout.)*

FLORA. With *me* in it. And Mrs. Grose and Miles— and you.   *(LIGHT #1. Desk dim.)*

MISS GIDDENS. *(Rising, taking FLORA by the hand)* Come along, then. *(They start towards the stairs.)* Once upon a time—once upon a time there was a ship called Bly—

FLORA. *(Sleepily)* That's the name of this house— I know—

MISS GIDDENS. *(Pausing at foot of staircase, looking up to ceiling as though she hears something there)* It was also—it was also the name of a very old ship— *(As they go upstairs)* This ship had long corridors and empty rooms and an old square tower—just like this house. It had a crew. Their names were— Do you know what their names were?

FLORA. *(Sleepily)* What were they?

MISS GIDDENS. *(As they reach the landing)* Why, their names were Flora and Mrs. Grose and Miss Giddens—and, yes, still another—and *his* name was Miles. *(They enter room off landing.)*

> *(MUSIC C. Volume 6. Exit platform—dim up, LIGHT #2. MUSIC volume to 45 as lights dim.)*

(Immediately, as MISS GIDDENS says "Miles," a thin vibration comes from far away—more of trembling of all inanimate things than of sound itself—and with this vibration, the SHADOW again appears at the window, filling the window, blocking out the

moonlight, almost as though about to enter the room as—)

SLOW DIMOUT

(MUSICAL transition to Scene III.)

ACT ONE

SCENE III

(Curtain up. MUSIC fade. LIGHTS up.)

SCENE: *The following morning.*
   It is a clear, beautiful day. The French door is wide open. The garden is apparent by its reflected light, green and cool, that fills the room.
   MRS. GROSE *is polishing the furniture. After a moment, she reaches into one of the pockets of her apron, pulls out two letters, places them on desk, looks out into the garden, then continues with her polishing.*
   FLORA *comes through door on landing and, unnoticed by* MRS. GROSE, *comes down, half-way, to sit on a stair. Her chin in her hands, she watches* MRS. GROSE *quietly.*

(MUSIC out.)

FLORA. *(Softly)* Where is Miss Giddens?
MRS. GROSE. Ah! Miss Flora! You startled me! Aren't you supposed to be in the schoolroom, now? Miss Giddens won't like it—and on her second day here, too—
FLORA. *(Undisturbed)* I finished my writing. Where is she?
MRS. GROSE. Picking some flowers—though I'm sure

she'd stop if she knew you weren't doing what she told you to do. You get back now, there's a lamb.

FLORA. *(Patiently)* But I've finished my writing—then I copied out a rhyme I knew by heart:

> In sleep she seemed to walk forlorn,
> Till cold winds woke the gray-eyed morn
>   about the lonely moated grange.
> She only said, "The day is dreary,
> He cometh not," she said;
> She said, "I am aweary, aweary,
> I would that I were dead."

MRS. GROSE. *(Appalled)* What was she thinking of to have you learn that!

FLORA. She gave me O's to copy—but *they* were so easy—

MRS. GROSE. *(Beneath her breath)* Then it's clear from whom you learned *that*, Missy! *(Flicks angrily at her desk)* And there's no telling what else!

FLORA. Are you dusting the ship, Mrs. Grose, dear?

MRS. GROSE. *(Grimly)* I'm dusting a desk—a ship, indeed!

FLORA. Miss Giddens says Bly is a ship—

MRS. GROSE. Then *you'll* get sea-sick, no doubt!

FLORA. O, no. But Miss Giddens was.

MRS. GROSE. *(Across room, dusting spinet)* Ah, Miss Flora—

FLORA. Well, *I* thought she was, for she came upstairs and I wasn't asleep, though I kept my eyes shut—and I heard her say: "Flora? Flora, dear?" And she could hardly get her voice out, so I expect she *was* sick, for she was very restless all night. I heard her.

MRS. GROSE. *(Laughing in spite of herself)* Miss Flora!

FLORA. *(Laughing with her as she comes down stairs, goes to French door)* So I *should* find her—for she may have fallen down— *(Goes out into garden.)*

MRS. GROSE. *(Laughing with amazement)* Fallen down, indeed! "Are you dusting a ship!" *(A moment passes, then, as* MISS GIDDENS' *approach is heralded by her shadow at the window.)* What a lovely day, Miss!

MISS GIDDENS. *(Entering from garden)* Yes, it is.

MRS. GROSE. Didn't you get the flowers, Miss? The vases are filled for them—

MISS GIDDENS. No—I forgot them— *(Crosses to staircase. Stops. Turning back to* MRS. GROSE) Mrs. Grose—?

MRS. GROSE. Yes, Miss?

MISS GIDDENS. Mrs. Grose—you know where the path ends in a clump of elms, beyond the lawn, close to the woods?

MRS. GROSE. Yes, Miss—

(MUSIC D. Volume 6.)

MISS GIDDENS. *(Lost in what she describes)* I was standing there—I was about to pick the flowers—but, suddenly, I felt that I was being stared at. I turned, expecting to find that it was you or Miss Flora who had come to call me— Instead, I saw a man, a stranger—who stared at me, Mrs. Grose—who stood there, casually, as though he belonged here—

MRS. GROSE. You're sure, Miss, it wasn't the gardener or his boy?

MISS GIDDENS. No one I knew. *(Trying to laugh)* I stood there waiting for him to approach me. I was sure of a reason for his being there and so I waited—and he —he waited with me—not coming closer—standing there, fifty yards away, though it seemed that he was as near to me as you are— *(She shakes her head as though to rid herself of the thought)* And then, even though there was that distance between us, I could feel his eyes on me—bold, insolent— He stared at me as though *I* were being *indecent*— I felt as though I was looking into someone's room— He stared at me, Mrs. Grose, as though *I* were the intruder! *(She laughs weakly.)*

(MUSIC 9.)

MRS. GROSE. And he is gone, Miss—?

MISS GIDDENS. O, yes! He went away—as casually as he had come—though, for all I know, he might be

still in the garden, somewhere, or in the woods— And the ridiculous thing, Mrs. Grose, is that only now am I angry! Not when I was *there*, mind you, when I might have questioned him—but now, when I am *here*—quite safe from him—I feel angry—and—a trifle ill— *(She shakes her head again and moves towards the desk.)*
(MUSIC out.)

MRS. GROSE. *(Staring at her)* But, Miss—

MISS GIDDENS. *(Disturbed—not wanting to go on with it)* Don't be concerned for me—I didn't sleep well. Let us forget it.—I see there are letters for me.

MRS. GROSE. Wouldn't you like some tea, Miss—?

MISS GIDDENS. *(Who has quickly, nervously opened the first of two letters)* It's from my youngest sister— and here— *(Turning to* MRS. GROSE, *a picture in her hand)* —here—she has sent a picture that I forgot to bring with me—of my family. I've never been without it—and yet I forgot it—and so she sent it— *(Gives* MRS. GROSE *the picture, starts opening the second letter.)*

MRS. GROSE. *(Looking at the picture)* How you must miss them—! Is this your first time away from them, Miss?

MISS GIDDENS. *(Frowning at letter in her hand)* Yes. How like their uncle. He's forwarded this letter without even opening it. It's from Master Miles' school. Their uncle has written on the back—"whatever it is, deal with it. Don't bother me with it. Not a word."

MRS. GROSE. O, that's his way, Miss. He never did like being bothered. What a pretty picture this is. A big family is what I like. Let them muss the furniture up a bit, I say. A scratch won't hurt here and there if there's happiness in a house—

MISS GIDDENS. *(All her uncertainty returning)* What am I to do? How am I to deal with this?

MRS. GROSE. With what, Miss?

MISS GIDDENS. Master Miles. He's been dismissed from school.

MRS. GROSE. *(After a long pause)* Dismissed—

MISS GIDDENS. Sent home.

MRS. GROSE. *(Blankness)* But aren't they all—?

MISS GIDDENS. Only for the holidays. Miles can't go back—at all.

MRS. GROSE. What has he done—? *(As* MISS GIDDENS *hesitates)* Is he really *bad?* Do the gentlemen say so?

MISS GIDDENS. They go into no details—they simply express their regret. They say it is impossible to keep him—

MRS. GROSE. Why?

MISS GIDDENS. That he is an injury to the others.

MRS. GROSE. It's too dreadful to say such cruel things! See him first, Miss, *then* believe it if you can! You might as well think ill of Miss Flora, bless her!

MISS GIDDENS. O, I know that, Mrs. Grose—but what am I to do? Am I to question him when I meet him at the coach this afternoon?

MRS. GROSE. This afternoon—?

MISS GIDDENS. Yes— Shall I put it to him?—boldly?

MRS. GROSE. See him first, Miss, before you think badly of him— It's cruel—too cruel—to write things like that about him!

MISS GIDDENS. You've never known him to be bad?

MRS. GROSE. Never known him— Oh I don't pretend *that!*

MISS GIDDENS. You like them with the spirit to be naughty? So do I. But not to the degree to contaminate.

MRS. GROSE. To—?

MISS GIDDENS. To corrupt.

MRS. GROSE. *(Laughing oddly—with a bold humor)* Are you afraid he'll corrupt *you?*

MISS GIDDENS. *(Wryly)* What a comfort you are— If I'd had a good night's sleep I'd be able to think this out and not be silly about it— But I didn't sleep—

MRS. GROSE. Miss Flora said that.

MISS GIDDENS. Did she? I hardly thought—

(WARN Curtain.)

MRS. GROSE. And that you bent over her and spoke her name.

MISS GIDDENS. Yes—because— *(Checks herself)* I wondered if she were thirsty—

MRS. GROSE. *(Gently)* Why didn't you call me—if you were taken ill?

MISS GIDDENS. Ill? Why, no. It was my first night here—that was all. After my home, small, crowded, this house with so many rooms empty—all shut up—so quiet and— *(There is a deadly stillness before she speaks again.)* And—I seemed to hear someone walking beneath my window— *(Covers her eyes with her hand)* I mustn't think about it— It's odd, though— I can't get it out of my mind— He stared at me so boldly— I could feel an intense silence into which all the sounds of the garden dropped—leaving me, as he walked away, with nothing to stare at but emptiness— Then—the smell of flowers—overpowering— *(She sways as though about to fall. CHIMES.)* I—I must go to Flora, now— *(Starts to climb stairs.)*

MRS. GROSE. *(With a sudden realization)* She's not up there— Miss—

MISS GIDDENS. *(Turning to her)* Where—then? *(As* MRS. GROSE, *frightened, looks towards window)* In the garden—?! *(She runs across the room, to the window.* MRS. GROSE *follows her, quickly.)* Flora! *(Exits out window)* Flora! *(MUSIC E. Volume 8.)*

MRS. GROSE. Miss Flora! Miss Flora! Miss Flora!

(FLORA enters door Left and goes to window.)

MISS GIDDENS. *(Off)* Flora! Flora!
(LIGHTS dim. MUSIC volume 45.)

CURTAIN

ACT ONE

SCENE IV

(MUSIC volume to 8. LIGHTS up.)

SCENE: *Twilight (same day).*
  The window is open. The lamps are not lighted, for the day has not quite passed, though the golden afterglow that fills the room will soon fade.
  This moment of twilight is silent but anticipates the break that soon comes from the garden.

FLORA'S VOICE. *(From the garden)* We're here, Mrs. Grose! Mrs. Grose! *(Entering. Running across to door, Left)* Miles! Miles is back!

MRS. GROSE. *(Off Left)* Here I am, lamb!

FLORA. *(Turning again to window)* Hurry! He's grown—he's so tall! You won't recognize him! *(Running to window)* The darling boy! O, hurry! Please hurry, Mrs. Grose!

MRS. GROSE'S VOICE. *(Off Left)* I am—I'm doing the best I can—bless you!

FLORA. *(Running out to garden)* Miles! Where are you, Miles? Don't hide from me, now! Where are you! *(Her voice dies away in the distance.)*

MRS. GROSE. *(Off Left)* O, dear! I'll be out directly! *(MUSIC out. As MRS. GROSE enters from Left, MISS GIDDENS out. MISS GIDDENS appears at the window. MRS. GROSE stops as she sees MISS GIDDENS)* Well, Miss? Master Miles?—where is he?

MISS GIDDENS. *(Flatly)* Somewhere in the garden. He ran off amongst the trees.

MRS. GROSE. *(Sensing the tension in MISS GIDDENS)* It *is* all right, isn't it, Miss? I mean—what did he say to you?

MISS GIDDENS. *(Coming into room)* About the

reason for his being sent home? Nothing. Nothing seems to bother him.

MRS. GROSE. You see? I told you there would be no trouble about it —*(Starts towards window.)*

MISS GIDDENS. I *don't* see. *(As* MRS. GROSE *stops)* We sat across from each other in the carriage and he was all smiles and not in the least concerned, if that's what you mean. Other than that—

MRS. GROSE. But you *do* like him?

MISS GIDDENS. O, he's charming. I expected, at least, that he'd be uneasy—that he'd say something about his school—

MRS. GROSE. *(Pleading)* But he's just come home, Miss. It'll come out. He'll tell you. I know he will—

MISS GIDDENS. O, no. I'll have to get it out of him.

MRS. GROSE. And it'll be nothing at all!

MISS GIDDENS. Then why hasn't he said something?
                                    (MUSIC F. Volume 9.)

(At this moment, MILES *appears at window. He is twelve years old; a handsome child whose face reflects a remarkable innocence, whose bearing is gentlemanly and proud. He looks at* MISS GIDDENS *then, with a great smile of welcome, goes to* MRS. GROSE.*)*

MRS. GROSE. *(Embracing him)* Master Miles—dear Master Miles—

FLORA. *(Running in from garden. Sits on ottoman)* O, there you are! I looked all over the garden for you! *(Fondly)* Why do you tease me so!

MILES. *(Looking at* MRS. GROSE *as she releases him)* You look as though you like to cry. Aren't you glad to see me?

MRS. GROSE. I'm that happy—I—

FLORA. She means she's so happy she could weep! But *I* was sick when I heard you were coming! My stomach turned over.

Miss Giddens. *(Sharply)* Is supper ready, Mrs. Grose?

Mrs. Grose. *(Startled)* Why—yes, Miss.

Miss Giddens. *(Coldly)* You must be hungry, Miles.

Miles. *(Sits on ottoman)* Yes, thank you, Miss Giddens.

> *(Stage area dim. LIGHT #1. MUSIC F continued.)*

Flora. Just think, Mrs. Grose—Miles ate four little cakes on the coach! And a wheel came off!

Mrs. Grose. *(Softly)* Did it, now?

Miles. *(Looking about the room. Completely at ease)* No. It almost did. A man fixed it and then we went along beautifully.

Mrs. Grose. Four cakes—and *I* made a pudding for you—

Miles. I actually ate only two. A little girl ate the others and her mother became quite angry. So I fibbed.

Miss Giddens. *(Sharply)* Why, Miles?

Miles. O, because the lady wouldn't scold *me*. So, of course, I *said* I'd eaten *four*. So you see, Mrs. Grose, I shall be able to enjoy your pudding.

(The light from the sky dies away with Miles' last words. The room is in darkness.)

Flora. Hello!

Miles. Hello!

Miss Giddens. *(Takes off her hat)* Flora, wouldn't you like to go with Mrs. Grose—and have her give you a taper—then you could light the lamps?

Flora. May I?

Miss Giddens. And Mrs. Grose, would you see to supper?

Flora. *(Still plaintively)* And may I have supper with you and Miles?

Miss Giddens. I don't see why not.

Flora. *(Following Mrs. Grose, who goes silently to*

door Left) And may Mrs. Grose have supper with us?

MRS. GROSE. Dear me, that wouldn't—

MISS GIDDENS. That *would* be nice.

(MUSIC F continued.)

FLORA. *(Taking* MRS. GROSE *by the hand)* She shall. Won't you?

MRS. GROSE. *(Hardly audible—as they exit Left)* If you'd like it, Miss Flora— *(Exits.)*

MISS GIDDENS. (MISS GIDDENS, *now that she is alone with* MILES, *seems filled with indecision. She turns to desk, places her hat upon it, opens the drawer, shuts it, then turns to him. Too casually)* Well, Miles? Don't you want to tell me something?

MILES. *(Returns her look with a charming smile)* Something?

FLORA. *(Entering Left with a lighted taper in her hand)* Do I look like an evening star? *(She doesn't seem to notice the silence between* MILES *and* MISS GIDDENS) We'll all have stomachaches, I'm sure. I saw the pudding and it's beautiful.

MILES. *(Going over to her, his hands in his pockets)* I shan't.

FLORA. *(Beaming at him)* No. You *never* do. I don't see how you manage not to—what with third helpings and all. *(A close intimate companionship exists between them. As though they deliberately ignore her,* MISS GIDDENS *is left on her own; she is aware of this —she involuntarily moves out of their way as they approach the desk* MILES *steps forward and lifts the globe from the desk lamp, gallantly.)* Thank you. If I have *even* a second helping I almost *die.*

(Desk area dim up. LIGHT #2.)

MILES. *(Smiling at her)* Silly. *You* dislike second helpings?

FLORA. *(Beaming at him as he replaces globe on lamp)* O, no. I love them.

MISS GIDDENS. Miles.

FLORA. *(As though* MISS GIDDENS *weren't in the room)* I shall die of them one day, of course. But I do think it'll be worth it— *(Lighting lamp—then blowing out flame of taper)* Especially if it's *pudding*. Not the soggy kind, you know— *(Places taper on desk, takes* MILES *by the hand. Together they go to staircase.)* The chewy kind—with raisins in it—

MISS GIDDENS. *(Firmly)* Miles.

MILES. *(Turning on first step—all smiles)* I should wash my hands for supper, shouldn't I?

(MILES *and* FLORA *run, silently, up the stairs and through door on landing.* MISS GIDDENS *looks up at landing as a burst of laughter comes from the room behind the door. Then she angrily sits down, opens desk-drawers, takes the letter out, rapidly reads through it. With sudden decision, she begins to write. A few moments pass. She rises, goes to French window, closes it but does not draw the curtains; she returns to desk, continues writing.* MILES *comes through door on landing and down the staircase.)*

MILES. *(Halfway down)* Am I disturbing you, Miss Giddens?

MISS GIDDENS. *(Pretending disinterestedness)* Not at all.

MILES. Flora's hiding.—When she's hidden, I'm to find her.

MISS GIDDENS. *(Writing)* Well, don't be too noisy.

MILES. (MILES *goes to French window. Looks out into garden over which complete darkness has fallen. After a moment)* It must be nice out in the garden, now—

MISS GIDDENS. *(Not looking up)* Too dark to be pleasant.

MILES. I'm not afraid of the dark. Are you?

(MUSIC F continued.)

MISS GIDDENS. *(Taken aback—looking at him)* Sometimes—

MILES. Why?

MISS GIDDENS. There's nothing to be afraid of, really—

MILES. I know that. Why are you afraid?

MISS GIDDENS. I suppose—I suppose I'm timid.

MILES. *(Seriously)* You shouldn't be. Everything's the same at night as it is by day. You're in a room and it's dark—so you light a lamp and—there's nothing but chairs and tables! Just as there always were!

(He gives a delighted laugh. MISS GIDDENS is finding it difficult to retain her anger against him.)

MISS GIDDENS. *(Looking up at him)* If everything were as simple as that—

MILES. But it is! Though grownups don't see it—usually. On the coach, the little girl's mother was nervous about the wheel—not while it was about to fall off—but after it was fixed. She said she was going to faint!—All because the wheel might have come off—which it *didn't!* You see? It's all in what you *think* might happen. Most of the time it doesn't.

MISS GIDDENS. *(Touches him on the arm)* Miles—

FLORA'S VOICE. Miles!

MISS GIDDENS. Sometime—we must talk about— *(She smiles at him—then she shakes her head)* Not now, though.

FLORA'S VOICE. I'm hid, Miles!

MILES. You don't suppose I might stretch my legs a bit out there, do you?

MISS GIDDENS. And disappoint Flora who's hidden and waiting?

MILES. No—I couldn't do that, could I? *(He goes across to stairs.)*

FLORA. Miles!

MILES. I'm coming. *(As he starts to climb stairs, smiling at MISS GIDDENS)* I'm glad you're here, Miss Giddens. I'm sure we'll get along splendidly together—I'll catch you! *(Goes off, into room on landing.)*

(LIGHT #3. MUSIC out.)

(Miss Giddens *picks up the letter she has started,
looks at it, begins to tear it up.)*

Mrs. Grose. *(Entering from Left. She is carrying
a small bag and some books)* Here are Master Miles'
books, Miss—

Miss Giddens. *(Rising quickly from the desk)* I've
been stupid, Mrs. Grose—how could I have been so
stupid? You were right—I should have given him a
chance— Well, I shall!

Mrs. Grose. You've spoken to him, Miss?

Miss Giddens. Not about his school—not yet. How
could I have made up my mind so quickly about him—
I who have brothers? When I think of the rage I felt
toward him fifteen minutes ago! O, a fine governess I
make, Mrs. Grose!

Mrs. Grose. What will you say, then?

Miss Giddens. In answer to the letter? Nothing until I've spoken to Master Miles.

Mrs. Grose. And to his uncle?

Miss Giddens. O, I shan't bother *him*—I'll handle it
myself. Master Miles will help me— He's an intelli-
gent boy— I've been so unfair to him! Meeting him
at the coach with what amounted to a stony silence—
Well— *(Laughs)* He'll have his chance to tell *his* side
of the story— Then, we'll see—

Mrs. Grose. *(Close to tears—but smiling)* Miss—
Would you mind, Miss—?

(They embrace, then Mrs. Grose *exits Left.)*

Flora's Voice. *(From room off landing—shrieking
with laughter)* O, Miles! How did you find me?

Miss Giddens. *(Smiling. Going to staircase)* Flora—

Flora. *(Coming onto landing)* Yes, Miss Giddens?

Miss Giddens. Don't get so excited, dear.

Flora. How can I help it? Miles is so clever at finding me out. Now he's hiding— *(She listens—then in a
whisper)* I hear him rustling—which means he's pre

tending he's getting under the bed. But he won't. He'll be somewhere else—and I'll *never* find him— It's quite frightening!

MISS GIDDENS. *(Laughing)* To know someone's there, in the room with you, and yet you can't see them? But that's the fun of it!

FLORA. You hear them breathing *right* behind you—but you don't dare turn around to look—!

MISS GIDDENS. And when you do they're not there at all!

FLORA. You find them when you least expect to!

MISS GIDDENS. They jump out at you!

FLORA. A terrible thing! But such fun! *(As MISS GIDDENS, laughing, goes to draw curtains at window)* Poor Miss Giddens— Do you feel better now?

MISS GIDDENS. *(Taken aback—not drawing the curtains)* Better—?

FLORA. You know—about everything.

MILES' VOICE. *(Calling)* Flora!

FLORA. *(Running off, into room off landing)* O, I'll never find you! *(MISS GIDDENS stares after her, frowning.)* I've found you! I've found you!

> *(MUSIC G, volume 6.)*

(MISS GIDDENS crosses room as though to go upstairs. But as she reaches stairs she comes to a sudden stop. She does not turn, but she is fully aware of the MAN who has appeared, framed in the window, staring in from the garden. His face is close to the glass of the window. Slowly, MISS GIDDENS turns to face him across the room. MUSIC up, volume 15. She does not cry out, nor does she move until the MAN steps backwards into the darkness of the garden. For a moment after he has gone, MISS GIDDENS remains still, then she runs to window, opens it and goes out into the garden after him. MUSIC out. There is an absolute silence for a long moment. MRS. GROSE enters room from door Left. She comes to an abrupt stop, her hand covers

her mouth to stifle a scream—for
has re-appeared in the window,
blank terror apparent in her face.)

MRS. GROSE. What—what in the name of good
the matter?

MISS GIDDENS. He was here—again.

MRS. GROSE. Who, Miss—?   *(WARN Curtain.)*

MISS GIDDENS. He stared in at the window—just as
he did in the garden this afternoon —He stared—only,
this time, he looked right past me as though he were
looking for someone else—

(Shrill, excitable laughter comes from MILES and
FLORA as they play in their room beyond the land-
ing. MISS GIDDENS looks up at the landing.)

MRS. GROSE. Do you fear for them?

MISS GIDDENS. Don't *you?*

MRS. GROSE. *(After a long moment)* But—what is
he like?

MISS GIDDENS. No one I've seen around here— *(Sits
on ottoman)* He has red hair—very red, close and curl-
ing. A long pale face. His eyebrows are dark—dark
and arched. His eyes seemed sharp—strange—awfully.
I only know clearly that they are small and—very fixed.
(MRS. GROSE *stares at her with a horror that grows as
she continues.)* His mouth is wide, his lips thin. He's
tall—erect—well dressed, but certainly not—a gentleman—

MRS. GROSE. *(Gasping)* A gentleman? Not he!

MISS GIDDENS. You *know* him?

MRS. GROSE. *(Almost a whisper)* Quint.

MISS GIDDENS. Quint?

MRS. GROSE. Peter Quint. His own man, his valet,
when the Master was here. When the Master left—
Quint was alone—

MISS GIDDENS. Alone?

MRS. GROSE. Alone with us— In charge.

lied.

ne 10 to 45.)

Scene V

(Curtain up. MUSIC volume to 8. LIGHTS up.)

Scene: *The following morning.*
It is a bleak and rainy morning. A cold, grey light comes from the garden in which, no doubt, every twig on every tree is dripping.
Miles and Flora are seated at desk—facing up. They are hard at work at some task set them by Miss Giddens.
Miss Giddens is seated on ottoman. She is working on some embroidery which is stretched before her on a frame. On the ottoman, beside her, lies a small box of pencils, schoolbooks and a large pin-cushion. Every now and then she looks up to stare at one corner or another of the room. Every stab of her needle shows the tension under which she now lives.
The only sound is the high, thin scratching of slate-pencils on slates as Miles and Flora do their task—a nerve-racking sound—a sound that is heard before the lights come up and that continues with nailbiting insistency.
Miss Giddens presses her hand onto her forehead.

FLORA. *(Looking at* MISS GIDDENS) Why are you doing *this—? (She repeats* MISS GIDDENS' *gesture)* You looked as though you were pushing something away— *(She goes to window, wipes a pane vigorously.)*

MISS GIDDENS. Flora. Sit down.   *(MUSIC out.)*

FLORA. *(Looking out into garden)* O, look! There's a bird with an enormous worm! Mayn't we go out?

MISS GIDDENS. *(Sharply)* Certainly not. It's raining.

FLORA. O, no, it isn't. It's dripping from every twig and leaf and branch—but—

MISS GIDDENS. Will you sit *down?*

FLORA. Why, of course— *(Returns to desk immediately and absorbs herself in her task.—After a moment:)* O, Miles! Your pencil *does* have a *terrible* squeak!

MILES. I can't help it, you know—

FLORA. Can't you? I thought you were doing it on purpose.—I wish *I* could— *(She tries. Her slate-pencil snaps in two)* O, dear—

MISS GIDDENS. *Now,* what's the matter?

FLORA. It's my pencil—

MISS GIDDENS. You shouldn't bear down on it so. *(Reaching into box beside her)* Here's another.

FLORA. *(Going to her)* Does the squeak of Miles' pencil send shivers through you? It does through *me*—

MISS GIDDENS. *(Shortly)* No. *(Repenting)* I know it's a horrible day—but could you try and do your task?—quietly, dear?

FLORA. Does your head hurt, Miss Giddens? *(To* MILES) O, Miles—*poor* Miss Giddens.

MISS GIDDENS. *(Trying to laugh—failing miserably)* Flora—Flora, dear—my head doesn't hurt—

FLORA. *(Sitting on ottoman)* Doesn't it? *(Taking* MISS GIDDENS' *hand)* You're warm— Miles? I do believe Miss Giddens has a fever!

MILES. Has she? May I get you a cup of tea, Miss Giddens? Or a plaster?

MISS GIDDENS. *(Laughing—though nearer tears)* A plaster? Whatever for? I'm not ill—you dear things!

It's the rain—and not being able to go out into the garden—and tiring my eyes with—with *this*— *(She sticks her needle into the pincushion.)*

FLORA. Then, why do you bother about it if you don't like it?

MISS GIDDENS. *(Trying to laugh)* It's my task for the day—like your spelling and geography—though nothing seems to be getting finished while we go on about nothing—

MILES. It's the rain that does it. *I* know—because I'm all turned about when I wake up and find the sun isn't out—

FLORA. *(Excitedly)* I know! I know! *I* get a funny feeling that *something's* going to happen! I wait all day—but nothing *ever* does— It's so disappointing—what with having to stay in—

MISS GIDDENS. Well, you're *not* going out.

FLORA. Not even with a hat?

MISS GIDDENS. Not even with a hat.

MILES. Don't keep on at Miss Giddens like that, Flora. We must do what she wishes, you know—

MISS GIDDENS. *(Almost breaking down. Her hand going to her eyes—then quickly away)* I—

FLORA. Of course we must. *(Putting her arm around* MISS GIDDENS' *shoulder)* I'm being naughty, aren't I?

MISS GIDDENS. No— It is I who am behaving wickedly— What a grumpy old governess you have!

FLORA. *(Kissing her—with charming affection)* You're not grumpy at all! Is she, Miles?

MILES. Of course she isn't. Though I wouldn't wonder if she were—

FLORA. Nor would I—with *everything* so horrible.

MISS GIDDENS. *(Hardly able to breathe)* Horrible—?

FLORA. *(Softly)* Why, yes—you know. *(Smiling up at her)* The rain—Miles' squeaky pencil—and my naughtiness—why! I wasn't even trying to be good!

MISS GIDDENS. *(Almost crying with relief)* But you *are* good! You both are!

FLORA. Well, I *might* try a little harder, don't you

think? *(Disengages herself, gently, from* MISS GIDDENS' *arms. Goes to desk.)*

MISS GIDDENS. *(Rising quickly)* Why—no! Why should you? If it's gloomy outside—that's no reason why we should be gloomy here! Let's play!

FLORA. *(Delightedly)* Play?

MISS GIDDENS. Yes! Why not? We've worked—haven't we? Well, then— *(To* FLORA) *You* can choose the game!

FLORA. Hide-and-seek!

MISS GIDDENS. No!

(So sharp is MISS GIDDENS' *voice that* FLORA'S *hand goes to her own mouth as though she has screamed.)*

FLORA. *(In tears—looking down at floor—whispering)* I'm—sorry— I thought you said I could choose the game—

MISS GIDDENS. *(Going swiftly to her. Kneeling before her—taking her in her arms)* I did—-I did say that —and you may. But let's not hide from each other— Mrs. Grose has dusted and tidied all morning and it wouldn't be kind of us to—to untidy the room all over again—would it? And what's the fun of hide-and-seek if you can't pull the beds apart and hide in cupboards?

FLORA. *(Without spirit)* Then—*you* choose a game.

MILES. *I* shall.

MISS GIDDENS. You see, dear? Miles has an idea!

MILES. *(Rising from desk)* Dressing-up.

MISS GIDDENS. That's a wonderful game! I can remember "dressing-up" with my brothers and sisters on rainy days—why didn't I think of it! It's ever so much more fun than—well, than anything else I can think of! *We* used to pretend— O, a hundred things! Here—use my handkerchief, dear— *(Gives* FLORA *a handkerchief)* Kings and queens—beggars and thieves!

FLORA. *(Still crestfallen)* May we?

MISS GIDDENS. *(Rising to her feet)* Of course you may.

MILES. Come along, then, Flora— *(Takes her hand.)*

(They cross to staircase.)

MISS GIDDENS. Why—where are you going—?

MILES. *(At foot of staircase as* FLORA *continues up)* To dress up— Didn't you say we may?

MISS GIDDENS. *(Starting to follow them)* I'll--I'll go with you.

MILES. But then you'd know what we were—there'd be no surprise—

(He turns and goes up the staircase to FLORA, *who waits on landing. Together, they go into room, closing the door behind them.* MISS GIDDENS *remains at Center, unable to move. She keeps her eyes on landing. Not the slightest sound is heard; it is as though the trees in the garden have stopped dripping, as though the earth itself has stopped turning.)*

MRS. GROSE. (MRS. GROSE *enters from door Right. Staring at* MISS GIDDENS, *then up at landing. Softly)* Miss?

MISS GIDDENS. *(Not turning. Almost inaudibly)* I let them go—Mrs. Grose, I let them go—

MRS. GROSE. *(Still at door, Right)* Where, Miss—?

MISS GIDDENS. Up there— *(All the bleakness of the garden seems to come indoors.* MISS GIDDENS *covers her face with her hands. Her voice comes wearily)* I let them go— All morning I kept them with me. Now— I've let them go—

MRS. GROSE. Couldn't you stop them—?

MISS GIDDENS. *(Her hands dropping from her face)* How? What reason could I give them? I see a man at the window—I ask you who it is—you tell me who it *was*—that he is dead— *(Violently)* Last night it was as though a nightmare possessed me! It was a nightmare, I told myself—it would pass, it must pass! All the things I would have asked you had I been able—I couldn't come to you even when the children were in bed—I couldn't allow myself to think further—it was a nightmare! I told myself it would pass! But it is no longer dark—it is daylight. And I *know* it— A man, something that was a man, looked in at me *from its grave! (Her voice never rises above a harsh whisper)* Should I call them now? What shall I say to them?

MRS. GROSE. Miss—I—

MISS GIDDENS. *(Without interruption)* I can't go up after them! I made Flora cry because I wouldn't let her play hide-and-seek! Because I thought of them hiding—and of how I would go through the rooms and find each one empty! I would call to them—they wouldn't answer— They would be up there alone— What would come at them—first from one room and then—from another—? *(Terror) Why* has he come *back!* Do you think? *(Her words die away. She stares through the dimness at* MRS. GROSE. *Little but their faces can be seen—so feeble is the light from the garden—so strange at morning—so much more, this dimness, than that loss of light that comes from a cloud passing over the sun.* MISS GIDDENS *moves, slowly, across to* MRS. GROSE *until she is but a step from her)* Mrs. Grose— How did he die—?

MRS. GROSE. Quint? Quint died early one morning —on the road from the village. They said at the inquest that he had slipped on the icy slope. He had been drinking. There was a wound on his head—from falling, they said. But I saw him. It was I who found him. The wound was terrible. He had died in pain!—such pain. Miss!—It was there in his face. His eyes were still opened— It wasn't an accident. I knew it couldn't be—for there were things in his life that would have accounted for violence done him—

MISS GIDDENS. What things?

MRS. GROSE. *(Numbly—as though beaten)* Disorders— Secret disorders—vices I don't guess at—

(Again, the silence crowds the room.)

MISS GIDDENS. *(As though a great weight presses on her)* They have never mentioned the time they were with him—his name—

MRS. GROSE. Don't try them—don't try them, Miss—

MISS GIDDENS. Were they together—often—? Quint and Miles?

MRS. GROSE. *(Tremendous disgust bursting from her)* It wasn't *him!* It was Quint's own fancy! To spoil him! Quint was much too free!

MISS GIDDENS. *(As though struck in the face)* Too free with *him?* With that *child?*

MRS. GROSE. Too free with everyone!

MISS GIDDENS. Mrs. Grose!

MRS. GROSE. *I* knew it! But the Master didn't!

MISS GIDDENS. And you never told him?

MRS. GROSE. He hated complaints!

MISS GIDDENS. *I* would have told!

MRS. GROSE. I was wrong— I was wrong—but I was afraid—

MISS GIDDENS. Afraid? Afraid of what?

MRS. GROSE. Of Quint. No one could go against him. He fancied himself master. He used his position here to do what he wanted. O, he was handsome enough!— but evil—such power he had over people!—He was a devil—!

MISS GIDDENS. You were afraid of him! Not of his effect on the children? They were in your charge!

MRS. GROSE. No! They were not in mine! The Master hated complaints! If people were all right to *him*—he wouldn't be bothered with more! So Quint gave all the orders, even about them.

MISS GIDDENS. And you could bear it!

MRS. GROSE. No! I couldn't—and I can't now!

MISS GIDDENS. *(The thought striking her with tre-*

mendous power) Why has he come back?—Not—not—
(Stair area dim up. LIGHT #1.)

*(She turns, looks up at landing as the door opens slow-
ly. Through doorway steps* FLORA. *She has dressed
herself in what might have been a curtain once—
heavily brocaded cloth that gleams about her
shoulders, is caught at her waist by a ribbon to fall
behind her in a long train. She wears a pin-
cushion on her head. She steps, daintily, to the
top stair. As she reaches half-way down the
staircase,* MILES *appears on landing. He has
wound a sheet about his head to form a turban. He
bends down, gathers* FLORA'S *train to him and so,
moving slowly as though part of an outlandishly
costumed masque, they continue down the staircase. Not a sound comes from* MISS GIDDENS.*)*

(LIGHT on spinet area dim up.)
FLORA. *(At foot of staircase)* I have borrowed your
pin cushion, if you don't mind— *(Then she and* MILES
*bow low to each other and cross the room to the spinet.
LIGHT #2. MUSIC volume 7. THUNDER #1.*
FLORA *stops, listens, smiles)* Thunder— *(*MILES *bows
to her and, taking a taper from a box on the spinet,
lights it and applies the flame to the candelabra.)* Miss
Giddens, dear? Would you sit there? *(She makes an
airy gesture toward the love-seat.* MISS GIDDENS *and*
MRS. GROSE *obey silently. They sit, stiffly, hardly visible
in the light from the candelabra on the spinet.* MILES
arranges FLORA'S *train about her feet. They again bow
to each other.)* Now, I shall sing a song and Miles shall
play for me. *(*MILES *seats himself at the spinet, strikes
a chord.* FLORA, *very grandly, clasps her hands together
and sings:)*   *(MUSIC out.)*
          Once there was a merry king,
          Who had a face of blue—
          He lived in a room
          At the top of the stair

With his handsome daughters two-oo,
With his handsome daughters two.

The older girl was tall and broad,
The tallest girl was she.
She combed her hair
Each early morn
With the top of a chestnut tree-ee,
With the top of a chestnut tree.

The younger girl was small and thin,
The smallest girl was she—
She washed her face
In a walnut shell
And galloped away on a flea-ee,
And galloped away on a flea.

Now. Miles shall sing for you and *I* shall play.

(MILES *rises, bows to* FLORA, *dusts the spinet stool,*
helps her to it, and when she is seated, arranges
her train. He takes candelabra and holds it before
him. THUNDER #2. He then bows to MISS GID-
DENS *and* MRS. GROSE. FLORA *strikes a chord.)*
                              (WARN Curtain.)

MILES. *(Candelabra in his hand)*
      What shall I sing
            To my Lord from my window?
      What shall I sing?
            For my Lord will not stay—
      What shall I sing?
            For my Lord will not listen—
      Where shall I go?
            For my Lord is away—

      Whom shall I love
            When the moon is arisen?
      Gone is my Lord
            And the grave is His prison—
(He begins to move upstage. MISS GIDDENS *and* MRS.

GROSE *watch him without moving. A strange, low vibration begins; a discord of sound as though something is trying to enter the room—soft but persistent.)*

> What shall I say
>> When my Lord comes a-calling?
>
> What shall I say
>> When He knocks on my door?
>
> What shall I say
>> When His feet enter softly,
>
> Leaving the marks
>> Of His grave on my floor?

(He reaches window)

> Enter! My Lord! Come from your prison!
> Come from your grave!
>> For the moon is arisen!

(THUNDER #3.)

(As he sings the last line, he throws the window open. The silk curtains blow into the room. Stepping beyond the threshold, he remains there, framed in the window, looking off; the candles he holds flutter in the wind; the VIBRATION rises with the wind. He remains motionless there.)

MISS GIDDENS. *(Rising from love-seat, staring at him)* Mrs. Grose—! He knows! He *knows!*

(The VIBRATION stops abruptly.)

FLORA. *(Turning from spinet. A puzzled frown mixed with a strange half-smile on her face. Softly)* Knows *what,* Miss Giddens?   *(THUNDER #4.)*

SLOW CURTAIN

ACT TWO

Scene I

That night.

As MUSICAL INTRODUCTION fades, Flora *is heard singing as Curtain rises.*

Flora's Voice. *(From room beyond landing, singing)*
> O bring me a bonnet,
> O bring me a bonnet,
> O bring me a bonnet of bright rosy red—
> With white roses on it,
> With white roses on it,
> O bring me a bonnet to wear on my head—

(Halfway through song, LIGHTS come up. One lamp is lit. The curtains are drawn across window. Mrs. Grose *stands by spinet, looking up at landing, listening to* Flora's *song.)*

Flora's Voice. (Flora *laughs as she stops singing)* Isn't that a lovely song, Miss Giddens?
Miss Giddens' Voice. It is—· Now go to sleep—and don't pull the covers off. (Miss Giddens *appears on landing.)*
Flora's Voice. There's something dripping outside my window— Do come and see what it is?
Miss Giddens. It's just the rain.
Flora's Voice. Is it *still* raining? I don't suppose we'll be able to go to church—shall we?

46

MISS GIDDENS. I'm sure it'll have stopped by morning—

FLORA'S VOICE. There's a beetle crawling on my neck!

MISS GIDDENS. Goodnight, Flora.

FLORA. *(Coming on to landing)* Is the box with the golden key opened yet?

MISS GIDDENS. *(Starting down staircase)* I'm afraid not.

FLORA. I know what's in it.

MISS GIDDENS. *(Continuing down staircase)* You can tell me in the morning. Go to sleep.

FLORA. *(Leaning on banister)* I *am* asleep. I'm having a lovely dream. I'm on a ship called Bly. We're going through a terrible storm. The waves are washing over the decks and—

MISS GIDDENS. *(At foot of staircase)* Flora! Go—to—bed this instant—

(LIGHT #1. Exit LIGHT out.)

(FLORA goes into her room immediately, closes door.)

MRS. GROSE. *(Softly)* Well, Miss— ? *(As MISS GIDDENS looks at her)* Forgive me, Miss—but I thought, perhaps—whatever I may have said before—perhaps their uncle should be told—now— *(She falters.)*

MISS GIDDENS. *(From where she stands)* What should he be told, Mrs. Grose?

MRS. GROSE. I don't know for certain—but **you** would know what to say, Miss—

MISS GIDDENS. How—how would I say it?

MRS. GROSE. You could write him—

MISS GIDDENS. And what would *you* say?—in a letter?

MRS. GROSE. But it isn't my place, Miss—to write—

MISS GIDDENS. *(Intensely, but in a whisper)* Then put yourself in my place—understand what stops me. What would their uncle think if he should receive a tale of— After all—you haven't seen anything— What if *I* have been imagining things? Is there anything I could write that would make sense to him?

MRS. GROSE. Write, Miss. Ask him to come—

MISS GIDDENS. And have him laugh at me? *(Desperately)* I've taken it on—whatever it is—

MRS. GROSE. There's only one thing that matters—the children mustn't be frightened—if you won't write —then, take them away!

MISS GIDDENS. *(A small panic)* Where?

MRS. GROSE. Anywhere—away from here—

MISS GIDDENS. If I took them away what good would that do? I should have to bring them back—this is their home— What reason would I give their uncle for keeping them away—?

MRS. GROSE. He won't ask, Miss—

MISS GIDDENS. He would want to know *why*, if I kept them away!

MRS. GROSE. But we must protect them—

MISS GIDDENS. From what? From my imagination? What if I have been imagining things? Wouldn't it be better if *I* left?

MRS. GROSE. *(With horror)* You can't leave, Miss!

MISS GIDDENS. I'm not trying to run from it!

MRS. GROSE. You *can't* leave unless you take them with you—away from here—

MISS GIDDENS. What if they see him—and pretend they don't—

MRS. GROSE. You mustn't think that— They wouldn't—

MISS GIDDENS. This morning—

MRS. GROSE. That—it was a childish game—!

MISS GIDDENS. It seemed a *game* to you! Was it more than that? Am *I* wrong in believing it *more than that?*

MRS. GROSE. *(Bewildered, despairing)* More?

MISS GIDDENS. You saw—and *heard* Miles!

MRS. GROSE. Playing a game!

MISS GIDDENS. You said Quint spoiled him—was too free with him—

MRS. GROSE. You can't blame Master Miles for that! No one could go against Quint!

MISS GIDDENS. What *effect* did it have on him! ?

MRS. GROSE. *(She does not understand—but what she senses makes her protect* MILES—*always she believes him innocent)* On Master Miles? I saw nothing, nothing wicked in him— I've never said to you that I saw anything *bad*— I saw the restlessness in him, yes, to be with Quint—to talk to him—to ask him questions. *(Before* MISS GIDDENS *can speak)* But could you *blame* him for that? It was what *any* boy would feel having no father, needing a man's companionship— *Quint* encouraged him—

MISS GIDDENS. How!

MRS. GROSE. *(Unable to pull back)* How—? I— Taking him away from his lessons—continually— Taking him away for hours— *(Trying to clarify it to herself, excuse it)* Miss Jessel—*she* was the governess —*she* didn't forbid it— What could *I* do? I could only watch and yet do nothing—to see—as I saw, from early morning, the restlessness in Master Miles to—go out across the garden—with *him*—holding on to *his* hand and asking questions in a voice that came to me—clear as I stood at the window— I heard his questions—but Quint's answers?—I never heard *them.*—*His* voice kept low until it brought the child's down to a whisper —both figures moving away— And I unable to go after them— *(For a moment, her sobbing is the only sound.* MISS GIDDENS *seems held by the picture created.)* Miss Jessel—she didn't forbid it—and I—I was told—to mind my business—

MISS GIDDENS. Then—you *were* aware of—

MRS. GROSE. Nothing wicked in Master Miles!

MISS GIDDENS. *(The picture is complete for her, suddenly—it needs great control for her to be able to speak)* But you knew Quint for what he was! Couldn't Quint have corrupted Miles? And couldn't Miles have deceived you with pretended innocence! ?

MRS. GROSE. Fooled me—?

MISS GIDDENS. Would he have wanted you to know?

MRS. GROSE. Know *what*, Miss—!?

MISS GIDDENS. Whatever they were—the things that Quint told him— *(She stops in horror at what she suggested. She remains staring into space as though the thought holds her—as though she elaborates upon it within herself—until, whatever conclusion she has reached, it overpowers her. Weakly, spent with emotion)* I don't know— Am I wrong—? I don't know— I don't know—let me sit in your room for a while— *(She moves, slowly, to Left; MRS. GROSE follows her—not looking at her)* I must be careful— *(Reaches desk, picks up the lamp on desk)* I must be careful in what I think—

(They exit door Left.)

(LIGHT #2. MUSIC K, volume 8.)
(Stage area out. Exit light on. As room remains dark but for a faint grey moonlight from the garden, a SOFT MUSIC enters—a suave atonality—then a diminuendo until nothing but the loud TICKING of the clock is heard to sharpen each second that passes—then, clearly, the clock CHIMES two— and a silence follows—sudden and appalling. Exit LIGHT out. LIGHT #3. MILES closes door. From the landing a small whiteness passes onto the stairs and down to the room and across the faint light from the garden—it disappears in the shadows down Right—another whiteness descends the stairs. From the spinet comes a run of notes— then a quick brightness as a match is struck. LIGHT #3A. Spinet LIGHT dim up. In this light, FLORA becomes visible as she lights a candle on the candelabra and takes it with her to Center. She wears a long white nightgown. MILES comes from staircase. He wears long white nightshirt. He stops and sits on floor, Center. He is intent on something that he creates on the floor before him

—something that is soon recognizable as being the beginning of a house-of-cards. FLORA, *standing at his side, watches silently as the miniature paper walls rise—then she bends down, blows at them and they collapse. She and* MILES *laugh softly, and the building of the house starts again. They are playing a game, as children will, during forbidden hours, and their movements are unhurried and self-assured. In the small light of the candle, they seem self-contained, though, against the high walls and along the wide floor, their shadows are distorted and enormous as though other beings within the same room.)*

MILES. *(Softly)* There is some cake in the pantry—

(FLORA *smiles and nods.* MILES *moves, quickly and silently, to door Right and off.* FLORA *kneels before the cards strewn on the carpet—her left hand holds the candle above her head—her right hand shifts the cards. She brings one close to her, peering at it. GHOST LIGHT on. LIGHT #4. As she does this,* THE FIGURE OF A WOMAN *appears on the landing, Right—a woman dressed in deepest black—tall and rigid.* FLORA *carefully returns the card to its pack, slowly rises to her feet and, turning to landing, faces the* FIGURE *on the landing—stretching out her hand toward it. MUSIC out. As though in answer, a deep moan comes from the* FIGURE *on the landing—a wretched sound without pity for any—a sound which continues for a long moment. As this moan dies away* MISS GIDDENS *takes a single step into room from Left. She carries a lighted candle. She stares directly at the* FIGURE *on the landing, then at* FLORA. *She sways as though about to fall. The* FIGURE *moves away into the shadows of the landing and is no longer seen.)*

FLORA. (FLORA *turns slowly and kneels again before the cards, her candle held high—fully aware of* MISS GIDDENS. *Singing softly, in a monotone, as she picks up one card and then another*)
> The queen of hearts
> She made some tarts
> All on a summer's day—

MISS GIDDENS. *(Her voice thin and like the scratch of a nail)* Who is it—!

FLORA. *(As though startled—dropping the candle)* O—! I've burnt my finger! How you startled me, Miss Giddens, dear!   *(Ghost light out. LIGHT #5.)*

MISS GIDDENS. *(As if she wakes from a nightmare)* Who is it!

FLORA. It is I, Miss Giddens—and— *(She giggles)* —won't Miles be surprised— He's in the pantry—

MISS GIDDENS. Who is it!

FLORA. *(Gently)* It is I—Flora— We've been naughty, Miles and I—

MISS GIDDENS. Who was that!

FLORA. Where—?

MISS GIDDENS. On the staircase!

FLORA. *(Turning to landing—as though bewildered)* There? There's no one there— *(Looking at* MISS GIDDENS—*as though about to cry)* You're frightening me—

MISS GIDDENS. You're *not* frightened!

FLORA. *(Laughs delightedly)* O, you're teasing me—! *(Turning to* MILES *as he enters, Right, a plate of cake in his hand)* We're caught, Miles! Miss Giddens has caught us being naughty!
> *(Stair light dim up. LIGHT #6.)*

MILES. *(Smiling)* Is she very angry—?

FLORA. *(To* MISS GIDDENS, *who is standing rigidly)* You're not, are you? *(To* MILES, *who joins her, Center)* I don't think she is—she's still half-asleep, I expect—and she'd like to get—to bed—and—so should we—and— *(She looks longingly at the plate in his hands)* —we'd better not have any cake— *(Her voice dropping to a whisper)* I don't think she'd like it if we did— (FLORA *places plate on spinet) I've* been punished—I burnt my finger—

(They cross to staircase and begin to go up to landing. Miss GIDDENS stares at them as though she does not see them. She seems selfcontained in her terror and unbelief of what she has witnessed. They smile at her as they reach the top.)

FLORA. Good night, Miss Giddens—dear—
MILES. Good night, Miss Giddens—

(They exit upstairs—closing the door softly behind them—like the miniature figures of an old clock.)
(MUSIC L. Volume 8.)

MISS GIDDENS. *(For a moment, MISS GIDDENS does not move. Then her head cranes forward. Numbly)* Who was it—? *(She goes to foot of staircase. At the foot of the stairs she stops. She looks towards the window. There is nothing there but the pale moonlight, the far, nebulous distances of the garden. She moves to the scattered cards, Center, places the candlestick on the floor and kneels, slowly, beside it. Her hand moves against the cards. Whispers)* Who was it—? *(She rises slowly, goes to window—stands there, looking out to garden. Her hand goes up to curtain-cord. Soundlessly, she draws the curtains together, cutting off the pale light from the garden, shutting herself in with the candlelight and the deep shadows of the room. Whispers)* Was it—? *(She shakes her head—a quick movement, as though something has caught itself in her hair. Now, as she speaks, her voice is thin, questioning—her words are directed towards herself—starting in a low monotone. Her voice is that of a woman talking in her sleep, the broken sentences meaning little in themselves—but together, fragmentary yet composing a whole, filling the room with the completeness of a nightmare. Her body passes through all the extremes*

*of terror—from utmost rigidity to spasmodic trem-
blings)* I—I—I must sleep—I must sleep—I can't
sleep— *(Her movements take her to the desk)* I must
write—I must write— What shall I write—? What
shall I say—? I must *sleep*— I can't think— I must
write— *(Suddenly—running to foot of stairs—staring
up at landing)* Who was it—? *(She becomes rigid)*
Was it *she*—? *(She moves, stepping backwards to Center—her eyes never leaving the landing which, un-
touched by light, is an emptiness beyond the stairs.
MUSIC out. She suddenly collapses to her knees, her
hands saving the rest of her body from reaching the
floor. She picks up a card as though seeing it for the
first time. She drops it as if it were on fire. Her body
crouches down until her arms cover her head, her hair
touches the floor. No sound comes from her.)*

(FLORA *appears on the landing. Silently, swiftly she
moves down the stairs and to the window—almost
without disturbing the curtains; she gets behind
them. All at once, a high giggle is heard from the
window.* MISS GIDDENS *lifts her head as though
listening. She lifts herself from the floor. Her
movements are uncertain as she goes to the window. Then, sharply, she pulls at the curtain-cord.
The curtains part.* FLORA *is standing quietly, facing into the garden.)*

FLORA. *(Smiling at* MISS GIDDENS) Why, I thought
I saw you walking in the garden— *(She slips past* MISS
GIDDENS, *who makes no move to stop her, and goes
running across the room and up the staircase. No
sound from her as she goes into her room, closing the
door behind her.)*

(MISS GIDDENS *pushes at the window. It swings open.
The moonlight is brilliant, white but cold. It
floods the room, throwing* MISS GIDDENS' *shadow
far behind her. She steps backwards into the room*

*as the shadow of someone in the garden follows
her. At Center she stops. MILES appears at window. He is wearing his nightshirt—his feet are
bare—he remains on the threshold.)*

MISS GIDDENS. *(Her voice barely audible—unemo-
tional—with the personality—her words are merely
spoken)* How did you get into the garden—
MILES. *(Smiling, waiting a moment)* Through my
window.
MISS GIDDENS. And why did you go out— What
were you doing there—
MILES. If I tell you—will you understand? *(Smiles)*
I did it to have you do this—
MISS GIDDENS. Do what—
MILES. Think me, for a change, bad—when I'm bad
I *am* bad— *(Laughs softly.)*
MISS GIDDENS. *(Still in an unemotional monotone)*
And—how did you know I would find out—
MILES. Oh—I planned that with Flora. She was to
get up and look out—and you were to find her—and
you did, didn't you?
MISS GIDDENS. You didn't think that I might be dis-
pleased.
MILES. O, yes. How otherwise should I have been
bad enough? Are you angry?
MISS GIDDENS. Your feet are wet—you might catch
cold—you must go to bed—

*(She does not move, but still faces the window as
MILES comes from window and starts toward
staircase.)*

MILES. *(Stopping at stairs—turning to her slowly—
speaking in a voice that is low and seemingly gentle)*
Why don't you stop it?
MISS GIDDENS. *(Not turning—her voice still flat and
unemotional)* Stop what, Miles—
MILES. *(After a long pause)* What you are doing—

MISS GIDDENS. *(Not turning)* What am I doing, Miles—

MILES. *(Although he does not raise his voice there is a new sharpness in it)* For one thing, you're meddling— You can't stop me going out if I choose to— You're just a governess— Wouldn't it be better if you remembered that? *(Starts to move across to staircase, his voice now charming and casual. He laughs softly, charmingly)* It *is* difficult, isn't it? This whole situation? *(Reaches staircase—starts up it. Speaking over his shoulder)* Couldn't you write to my uncle? *(As* MISS GIDDENS *neither answers nor moves)* You can't, can you? He so *hates* being bothered— *(Stops and looks at her for a moment)* O, it isn't that I mind being with you and Mrs. Grose and Flora— *(Smiling)* I rather like it—and I do like *you*— *Turns and continues up to landing; on landing, he looks down at her and she, as though against her will, turns and looks up at him. He stares down at her, smiling)* But is it the best thing? Being with a governess all the time? *(Pause. Then, very softly, casually)* A boy wants other things, you know— *(He turns away, enters his room and closes the door softly behind him.)*

*(*MISS GIDDENS *remains in the strained, staring position she has taken. Her shadow curves and flickers in the candlelight—then, as though her body imitates the quivering of her shadow, she begins to tremble. Her mouth opens—no sound comes from her. She remains thus, caught within a palpitation of terror. Then, as though awakening from a nightmare, she screams:)*

(CHIMES.)

MISS GIDDENS. Mrs. Grose—! *(As she screams, the clock CHIMES the quarter-hour and, with this sudden sound, she moves—running to door, Left. She leans into the darkness, off)* Mrs. Grose—! *(As her screams die away, a silence falls for a moment—then the sound of the clock's TICKING seems to swell. She turns from the door. Her movements are mechanical, as though she feels the need of movement without reason. In the candlelight, she is a figure dwarfed by shadow without substance.* MRS. GROSE *enters from door, Left. She carries a candle; her hair is in two braids, a shawl is about her shoulders, she wears a nightgown, there are slippers on her feet. As* MRS. GROSE *enters,* MISS GIDDENS' *words come pouring from her—her voice rising and falling—questioning—not waiting for an answer.* MRS. GROSE *stands in stunned silence. She looks rapidly into every corner of the room)* Why have you kept it from me!

MRS. GROSE. Miss—*Miss*—I—

MISS GIDDENS. *What* have you kept from me? *(Twisting to look up at landing)* You must tell me— Miss Jessel—why did she leave! *(Turning again, to* MRS. GROSE) And—Miles— *(Going to* MRS. GROSE— *close to her)* I'll make you tell me!

MRS. GROSE. *(A deep emotion beneath the bewilderment)* What has she to do with Master Miles—?

MISS GIDDENS. *What* have you kept from me?

MRS. GROSE. Nothing— I promise you—nothing that could concern you—

MISS GIDDENS. Why did she leave!

MRS. GROSE. *(Against her will)* I thanked heaven she left—

MISS GIDDENS. Why! Why?

MRS. GROSE. *(Not understanding—against her will)* She couldn't have stayed— *(Returning* MISS GIDDENS' *stare)* You ask why I held back what I know? About *her?* Because I couldn't bring myself to think about her! When she left— *(Without interruption)* —when she left I wouldn't see her— Here—with two children! Not caring, you see! Thinking only of herself and of *him! (Disgust distorts her voice)* Using this house, every room—*any* room— I came upon them once in this very room, sitting together, laughing together loudly. And then at night the dreadful silence that toward morning was broken by her weeping. I would hear her walking through the halls calling his name. He did what he wished with her. She left to go home, she said. And then we heard she had killed herself.

MISS GIDDENS. *(Harshness and repulsion)* And yet you let the children be with them? You should have taken them away!

MRS. GROSE. *(Sobbing)* They were not in my charge— I was in no position—

MISS GIDDENS. *(Harshly)* What if the children were aware of the relationship?

MRS. GROSE. *No—!*

MISS GIDDENS. What if they used the children to hide what went on between them?

MRS. GROSE. *No*—Miss— *(WARN Curtain.)*

MISS GIDDENS. They made the children *lie* to you! How did they use them? What did they tell them, show them, *make* them do—!

MRS. GROSE. No, Miss—no—it's not possible—

MISS GIDDENS. *(It is as though she speaks in her sleep; she speaks not only to* MRS. GROSE, *but also to herself—questioning and answering. And* MRS. GROSE *listens as though she is caught by the same dream.)* She was here— *(MUSIC M. Volume 8. Looking at the floor, Center. She, slowly, looks up at landing)* —up there—a woman—Miss Jessel—her eyes fixed on Flora —fixed with a fury of intention—as though to get hold of her—to share with the child the torments she suffers. She's come back! *(Pause)* You don't believe me— Then ask Flora! *(Her hands over her face)* No—! She'll lie!

MRS. GROSE. *(With difficulty)* Miss—how *can* you!

MISS GIDDENS. *(Her hands drop to her sides)* And Miles— You should have heard him! Reminding me to keep my place!—not to *meddle*—in *what? (Looking up at landing)* The look he gave me as he reached the top of the stairs— *(Her head jerks away in revulsion)* It is difficult—even as one woman to another—to tell you what I felt as he stared down at me— He was not a child! I felt obscene.

MRS. GROSE. *(Going quickly to her)* Stop it, Miss—!
Stop it—! *(Takes* MISS GIDDENS *by the shoulders.)*

MISS GIDDENS. *(Pauses as though for breath. A long
drawn-out sigh comes from her—her voice is now piteous and pleading)* I am so tired— *(Slow CURTAIN
beginning. As* MRS. GROSE *again goes to her, takes her
arm, gently but with an emotion that is akin to fear)*
Dear God help me— I am so tired—

               (Go LIGHTS. MUSIC volume to 45.)

CURTAIN

ACT TWO

SCENE II

Curtain up. MUSIC fade. LIGHTS up.

SCENE: *The following afternoon. Sunday.*

    *Though it has not rained for hours, it is a grey
day. The curtains are pulled open, the Center
French window is open. Now and again, through
the scene, the light brightens and fades as clouds
move away from or crowd over the sun. The clock
CHIMES half-past one. A few moments pass.*

    MISS GIDDENS *appears on landing.*

    As MISS GIDDENS *reaches last stair,* MRS. GROSE
appears in garden, at window. She wears a bonnet; a shawl is about her shoulders.

MRS. GROSE. *(Enters room. To* MISS GIDDENS*)*
Good afternoon, Miss— *(She remains at window. She
is obviously uneasy—uncertain as to what should be her
next move)* I didn't wake you, Miss. I hope I did right.

MISS GIDDENS. *(Her voice is flat, unemotional)* I
heard you leave— I was not sleeping—I was writing a
letter.

MRS. GROSE. *(Waits a moment. Then, softly—sighing)* I am glad, Miss—

MISS GIDDENS. I have written to their uncle— I am resigning from this post—

MRS. GROSE. *(Coming towards her—anxiously)* Ah, Miss—

MISS GIDDENS. *(Flatly) You* suggested I should write—

MRS. GROSE. Only to have him come here—to have him help—

MISS GIDDENS. He could only ask me to leave— I am saving him that trouble— *(With tremendous control to keep herself from screaming)* The responsibility is too great—

MRS. GROSE. No, Miss, please—you can't—

MISS GIDDENS. *(Her voice under control)* —it is not an hysterical letter, Mrs. Grose— I shall wait for his answer— Then I shall leave— *(Desperately—though controlled)* I cannot stay here— (MRS. GROSE *is at a loss for words—but is obviously near to tears.)* Until I leave, I shall do my best—after that— Where are the children—?

MRS. GROSE. In the garden, Miss— I—

MISS GIDDENS. You *left* them—?

MRS. GROSE. *(Taken aback)* It isn't too damp, Miss. —They promised to keep near the house—and—

MISS GIDDENS. *(Harshly)* Tell them to come in—

MRS. GROSE. *(She stares for a moment at* MISS GIDDENS) Yes, Miss— *(To* FLORA, *outside window)* O, there you are. Miss Giddens wants you to come in. *(She turns abruptly away—goes to window and into garden.)*

FLORA. (FLORA *appears at window. She wears a bonnet, gloves, a neat Sunday-coat. She carries a hymnal in her hand. As she enters through window)* Very well. Miles and I were talking about the soloist. She had such a *squeaky* voice! Tra-la, she sang—but I thought she was choking. *I* wouldn't sing in a choir if I had a voice like that. Good afternoon, Miss Giddens—

MISS GIDDENS. Good afternoon—Flora— *(They remain where they are—as though each sizes up the other.)* Flora—

FLORA. *(Looking down at the floor. Quickly)* O, look —a dead beetle! *(Kneeling down to look)* You'd never know it was dead except that it's on its back and isn't kicking— Miss Giddens? Can you hear a beetle's heart beating?

MISS GIDDENS. No.

FLORA. Can't you? *I* can. This one is quite dead—it isn't trampled on or anything. It's just dead. Decidedly dead. Do you suppose it smells? *(She bends down until her nose touches the floor)* It doesn't.

MISS GIDDENS. Throw it outside—Flora—

FLORA. *(Picking up the beetle)* O, no! Mayn't I keep it? *(Rising quickly before* MISS GIDDENS *has a chance to speak)* I shall put it with my handkerchiefs and ribbons— *(Running to staircase)* Beetles don't decay, you know— *(Running up staircase)* They get drier and drier like a twig— *(Suddenly singing as she runs up to landing)*

> Beetles don't decay—
> Beetles don't decay—
> Beetles don't decay, my love,
> Beetles don't decay—

(She runs into room, off landing, leaving the door open.)

MISS GIDDENS. *(From Right of Center—again a strange panic begins to possess her)* Flora—!

FLORA. *(From her room)* I won't be long. *(Singing)*

> Choose a ribbon-blue—
> Choose a ribbon-red—
> Better choose a ribbon-black,
> For the beetle's dead—

O! Miss Giddens!

MISS GIDDENS. *(Unable to move—staring up to landing)* What is it!

FLORA. *(Her head appearing through door of her*

room) Another one! Another beetle! He was on my bed! Imagine finding beetles on Sunday! *(Her head disappears back into room. Singing)*

Beetles on Sunday!
Beetles on Sunday!
What a lovely thing to find
Two beetles on Sunday!

(Coming out to landing) There— They're tucked away in my ribbons. *(Running down stairs)* Mrs. Grose *hates* beetles. *(She stops—staring at* MISS GIDDENS *for a long moment. Then in an excited whisper)* Do you know what happened once?

MISS GIDDENS. *(Going to meet her—almost inaudibly)* Here—let me take off your hat—

FLORA. *(On lowest stair as* MISS GIDDENS *unties ribbons)* Once Mrs. Grose gave me some porridge and I ate all of it. And the last spoonful had a beetle in it! I chewed on it and I chewed on it and it tasted like twigs.

MISS GIDDENS. Let me take off your gloves—

FLORA. *(Stretching out her hand)* I said to Mrs. Grose: "O, look! I'm eating a beetle!" And she said: "Spit out the nasty thing, Miss Flora!" But I couldn't because I had swallowed it—and Mrs. Grose wouldn't believe it *was* a beetle—so I said: "Shouldn't *I* know how beetles taste?" And she got quite angry. *(As* MISS GIDDENS *suddenly kneels to pull her close and hold her tightly)* Why—you're crying— Miss Giddens, you're crying— Why are you crying? Are you ill, Miss Giddens, dear? You mustn't cry— It's not going to church that makes you feel that way, I expect— *(Pulling at* MISS GIDDENS *to make her rise—very gently)* We'll sit —over there —*(Nodding at love-seat)* And you may help me cut out pictures for my paste-book— *(She leads* MISS GIDDENS *over to love-seat—and* MISS GIDDENS, *sobbing with a low, dry sound, allows her, as though she has no will of her own)* Now—sit here and don't worry about a thing— (MISS GIDDENS *sits—her eyes tightly closed.)* When Miles and Mrs. Grose come

in we'll sing a song or two or maybe play a game—
quietly, as it's Sunday— *(Going to French window—
looking out)* I can see them—at the end of the garden.
Miles has lost his hat, I think—the careless boy—
(Pause) He's running away from Mrs. Grose and
she's having difficulty chasing him.—He's throwing
leaves at her, now— *(A strange, subtle sadness creeps
into her voice)* They're having fun—but so are we—
I don't wish I were out there. I'd rather be here with
you— *(Her hands are clasped behind her back—she
looks forlorn. Going to desk, pulling open a drawer,
taking a sheaf of pages and a scissors)* I haven't cut
out pictures since last summer— Now you can tell me
what they mean— Here's a picture of a porcupine—
but it says it's a "Hysterix cristata"— And here's a
lizard—but underneath is written "Lacerta Calotes"—
Why? Miss Giddens, why? *(She sits on love-seat—
frowning.)*   *(LIGHT #1. Stage area dim.)*

MISS GIDDENS. *(In a low voice—not opening her
eyes)* Those are Latin names—

FLORA. But *isn't* this a porcupine?

MISS GIDDENS. *(Opening her eyes to stare at page—
blankly—her mind filled with other thoughts)* Yes.

FLORA. Then I shall paste it in my book and write
"Porcupine" under it— *(She busies herself with the
scissors.)*

MRS. GROSE'S VOICE. *(Distantly—from the garden)*
Master Miles! Master Miles!

FLORA. Miles is being naughty. *(Continues to cut)* I
can't get all the bristles. They're too little. But they're
so many that I don't think one or two will matter. *(She
places cut-out beside her, carefully, and starts to cut
another)* If it's clear tomorrow may we go out on the
pond? It's pretty, though it's full of leaves and twigs—
There's a little boat tied under the willows. Miles used
to go there before he went away to school—

MISS GIDDENS. *(In a small, tight voice)* Alone?

FLORA. *(Intent on her cutting)* O, no. And he told
me he saw a hand waving on the bottom but Mrs. Grose

said: "Stuff and nonsense!" "Stuff and nonsense," she said!

MRS. GROSE'S VOICE. Master Miles! Master Miles!

MISS GIDDENS. *(Suddenly sitting up—her back rigid—her hands clenched in her lap—her voice sharp and cold)* With whom did Miles go?

(MUSIC N. Volume B.)

(FLORA stares at her—the light seeps away. Everything in the room seems to lose its solidity and to undulate as though under water.)

FLORA. *(Sharply)* O, dear! I know it's going to rain again! How dark everything's getting— I can hardly see—and it isn't even two o'clock. *(MUSIC out. The excitement that possesses a child when a thunderstorm is imminent seems to take hold of her. She scatters the pictures as she jumps up from love-seat)* I must cover my beetles, poor things! *(So quickly does she move that MISS GIDDENS has no time to stop her. She runs up staircase—singing as she runs:)*

> Beetles don't decay!
> Beetles don't decay!
> Beetles don't decay, my love!
> Beetles don't decay!

MRS. GROSE'S VOICE. *(Nearer now)* Master Miles! Master Miles!

FLORA'S VOICE. *(From her room off landing)*

> Choose a ribbon—blue!
> Choose a ribbon—red!
> Better choose a ribbon—black!
> For the beetle's dead!

(MISS GIDDENS does not call again—instead her eyes turn to look down Right, where, a part of the shadows, stands the FIGURE OF A WOMAN as though just entering. Rigidly, this silhouetted FIGURE remains facing upstage, its head tilted towards the landing on which FLORA now reappears—her eyes

*downcast as she steps slowly from one stair to an-
other. Her voice is low, as though she speaks to
herself.)*

FLORA. *(Softly)* The poor, poor things—thought I'd
forgotten them—thought I'd leave them there—getting
colder and colder—of course I wouldn't— *(Singing
softly, eyes still on her feet as she descends staircase)*
                    Put him in a box—
                    Put him in a box—
                    Put the beetle in a box—

MRS. GROSE. *(Appearing at French window. Breath-
lessly, as she enters room)* Master Miles has hidden
himself. Miss! I've called and I've called—and—

                                (WARN Curtain.)

MISS GIDDENS. *(Rising from love-seat in one movement. Forcing herself not to scream)* She's there—
she's there! (MRS. GROSE, *a step beyond threshold,
stops short. She stares at* MISS GIDDENS.) Flora!

FLORA. *(On last stair—staring at* MISS GIDDENS)
Yes—?

MISS GIDDENS. *(Rigid—before love-seat)* Look,
Flora!

FLORA. *(Her eyes fixed on* MISS GIDDENS) I—I don't
see anything—

MISS GIDDENS. There! There! There! You *see* her!
You see her as well as you see me!

FLORA. I don't—I don't see anyone—*really*—truly—
I don't— I don't see anyone— *(Screaming as she runs
across room to* MRS. GROSE, *who is staring, her hands
over her mouth, at the* FIGURE *down Right.)* I'm
frightened!

MRS. GROSE. *(Swiftly taking* FLORA *in her arms)*
She isn't there! Nobody's there! How can she be? She's
dead and buried! *(She faces* MISS GIDDENS—*all her
protective instincts towards* FLORA *blotting out her
terror.)*

FLORA. *(Her face distorted with hatred—her voice
choked and ugly—spitting the words at* MISS GIDDENS)

I see nothing! I never have! You're cruel! Wicked! I hate you! I hate you! I hate you! *(Burying her head against* MRS. GROSE*)* Take me away—take me away from her— She's cruel— Take me away from her— Take me away— Take me away— She's cruel— wicked— I don't want to see her again— I hate her— I hate her! *(MUSIC O. Volume 15.)*

(LIGHTS dim quickly, on FLORA'S *sobs, which rise as—)*

SLOW CURTAIN

ACT TWO

SCENE III

(Curtain up. LIGHTS up: MUSIC fade.)

SCENE: *Twilight. The same afternoon.*
The rain has passed, but through the window comes a sulphurous light, coming directly into the room, which seems to deepen the shadows of the far corners, to stress them so that the room is divided into shadow and substance. A strong WIND circles the house.
MISS GIDDENS is on the love-seat. MRS. GROSE comes from the room Left. She has a coat over her arm. She is dressed for travelling.
She is caught by the agitation of departure. Every moment she remains in the house is one of added terror.
She comes, quickly, down to the stairs. She speaks in a hushed voice.

MRS. GROSE. Miss? Miss Giddens? *(Up to window, looking out to garden)* Miss Giddens?
MISS GIDDENS. *(From love-seat)* I am here.
MRS. GROSE. *(Startled—turning to her)* The car-

riage is waiting, Miss— Everything we'll need is packed: we must leave, now—

MISS GIDDENS. And Miss Flora?—where is she?

MRS. GROSE. In my room— *(Embarrassed—but the importance of departure uppermost in her mind)* She is dressed and waiting—

MISS GIDDENS. But she won't come down?

MRS. GROSE. *(Near to tears—fumbling)* She will— when we are about to leave— I tried to get her to come to you—

MISS GIDDENS. *(Quietly)* But she wouldn't. I didn't expect her to.

MRS. GROSE. She will, Miss— It's only that she is afraid— She's frightened as long as she is in this house—

MISS GIDDENS. Frightened? That is anger, Mrs. Grose.

MRS. GROSE. Ah, Miss— If you could have heard her—

MISS GIDDENS. Crying? I did. And I heard you comforting her. I know all the tricks she must have played to get your sympathy.

MRS. GROSE. *(Tears)* It isn't that—it isn't. It's fear —so much fear in that child— She even made me promise—made me *lock* her in my room—

MISS GIDDENS. *(Quietly)* So that *I* could not get to her.

MRS. GROSE. But only because—because you might ask, again—

MISS GIDDENS. And because I wouldn't question her once we were in the carriage? I couldn't, could I?— With you there to stop me?

MRS. GROSE. I would have to. *(Desperation)* You are wrong about it—you couldn't be right— Thinking *that*—about her— *(With tremendous agitation)* Please, Miss— You will see—once out of this house—how wrong you have been —*(Looking down at the coat she is holding)* Here is Master Miles' coat— Where is he? He must put his coat on —We must leave, quickly—

MISS GIDDENS. He is in the garden.

MRS. GROSE. *(Turning to window)* He must put his coat on— The carriage is waiting—

MISS GIDDENS. He knows that.

MRS. GROSE. I shall call him— We must all leave, now—

MISS GIDDENS. He is hiding. He's been hiding ever since he came back from church. He won't come to you.

MRS. GROSE. *(Turning back—bewildered)* Then—*you* call him, Miss— The carriage is waiting—

MISS GIDDENS. He is not going.

MRS. GROSE. *(Not grasping it)* We *all* are—

MISS GIDDENS. He is staying here. With me.

MRS. GROSE. *(Unable to move)* Why—?

MISS GIDDENS. I think it best.

MRS. GROSE. *(Horror)* To keep him here? In this house?

MISS GIDDENS. You must take Miss Flora to her uncle.

MRS. GROSE. And not—Master Miles?

MISS GIDDENS. No. Not Master Miles.

MRS. GROSE. *(Desperation—horrified bewilderment)* Why? Why? You'd keep him here? Instead of taking him away? Why?

MISS GIDDENS. To face him with it.

MRS. GROSE. What you imagine? You'd face him with that?

MISS GIDDENS. *(Her control is wearing thin)* What *I* imagine? After what you saw this morning?

MRS. GROSE. Because of it—because of what I saw—we must take them away— *(Running to window)* Master Miles! Come in, Master Miles!

MISS GIDDENS. *(Raising her voice, but still with a tremendous control)* He won't come to you!

MRS. GROSE. *(Standing at window, her head bent, her whole body forced against her tears)* Make him!

MISS GIDDENS. He is hiding— I went looking for him— I called to him— Once, I thought I saw him, amongst the trees—spoke to him as if he *might* be there—telling him that I wanted to help him—asking him to come to me— There was no answer. Then I saw clearly—what I *must* do.

MRS. GROSE. And if he doesn't come—back?

MISS GIDDENS. The carriage will leave. He will think we've all gone. Then he will come to the house.

MRS. GROSE. If he does—how will you bring yourself to ask him— Can *you* face it? Not caring what you make a child meet with?

MISS GIDDENS. Not *caring?* You have seen—

MRS. GROSE. *(Violently—as credo)* Whatever I have seen—I cannot believe them part of it! That this house is filled with evil, yes, I believe that— But that the children are—? I cannot believe it! I cannot believe it!

MISS GIDDENS. They are.

MRS. GROSE. Take them away—let us take them away!   *(LIGHT #1. Stage area dim.)*

MISS GIDDENS. You can take Flora—she is young—she can be made to forget away from here— But Miles? Must end it here. It isn't easy for me—Mrs. Grose. I almost ran from it— I sat there and had my thoughts take hold of me so that I would have screamed had my breath obeyed me— All that was base in Quint lives in Miles. He lives with the memory, the longing for all that Quint taught him. I must free him of it. Even if I must hurt him.

MRS. GROSE. You'll drive him too far—! No child could survive such terrors—!

MISS GIDDENS. You will take Flora to her uncle. And you must give him my letter! I have written what I believe to be true. *(Searching desk drawer)* It isn't here—

MRS. GROSE. Think of the danger— Come away—

MISS GIDDENS. *(Blankly)* I put it here—in this drawer—

MRS. GROSE. Then where is it? No! He wouldn't do that—

MISS GIDDENS. *(Coldly, without emotion)* You shall have to tell their uncle— I know you will tell him the truth. As much of it as you understand. And, now, you must go. *(As though holding herself in readiness.)*

MRS. GROSE. *(As she goes, slowly, Left)* God help you. God help you both— *(Exits.)*
          (LIGHT #2. Stage area dim. MUSIC P. Volume 8.)

(MISS GIDDENS *does not move for a moment. Then she turns from the desk mechanically and goes to love-seat and sits there. Her face is expressionless. She is rigid, waiting. A low MUSIC is heard: A sonorous, slow-moving, passing-of-time. With this music the twilight fades—seeps away—until she can be barely seen. The strong clatter of carriage WHEELS passes through the garden and is gone. The high sound of insects toward night can be heard—and, always, the harmonies cross each other, until, as though MISS GIDDENS' thoughts merge into a single one, the CLOCK is heard, alone: A climax of whirring works before chiming— As the chimes die away, MILES appears at the window, dimly seen—enters room. He comes into the room—crosses—starts to climb stairs—stops.)*   *(MUSIC out.)*

MILES. Why are you sitting in the dark, Miss Giddens? I knew you'd still be here. *(She lights lamp. LIGHT #3. Stage area dim up.)* You know—I might have stayed out there, in the garden, quite a bit longer. —Only I thought of you sitting here. I thought: "How dull for Miss Giddens!" I thought: "Why, I'm not doing anything to amuse her!" Rude of me, wasn't it?— leaving you alone? But I won't anymore. *(Sits chair Right)* Well, here we are. The two of us alone. I hope you don't mind?

MISS GIDDENS. Being alone with you? Not at all. What else should I stay on for? Miles, I want to talk to you. *(She is afraid but does not show it)* Miles— You know—or perhaps you don't—but, this is the first position I have ever held—

MILES. *(Lightly)* It's been too much for you? But Flora's gone and you were her governess— So it's sort of a holiday for you, isn't it?—not having her here?

MISS GIDDENS. You—are still in my charge.

MILES. *(Laughing for a moment)* Actually, I'm not your responsibility, you know.

MISS GIDDENS. You might as well accept me as being in charge of you.

MILES. Does it make you happier to think that you are? *(With a little bow)* Very well, then, whatever you wish.

MISS GIDDENS. What were you doing in the garden?

MILES. Haven't you ever been in a garden?

MISS GIDDENS. Yes.

MILES. Well? *(Laughs lightly.)*

MISS GIDDENS. *(Pause)* Miles— You could help me by being honest.

MILES. I haven't lied—you haven't asked me anything I don't want to answer.

MISS GIDDENS. Are there such things?

MILES. You ask such funny questions! What was *I* doing in the garden. As though there were other things to do besides looking at or picking flowers or wading in the pond or climbing trees—

MISS GIDDENS. Then why didn't you come to me when I called you?

MILES. *(Amazement)* *Did* you? I *saw* you, you know. You were walking around, almost in a circle, looking from side to side as though you expected to meet someone—

MISS GIDDENS. Then why didn't you come to me!

MILES. I thought you wanted to be alone. I was quite close to you. I said: "Miss Giddens!"—in quite a loud voice—

MISS GIDDENS. That is not true! You never called to me! I should have heard you!

MILES. *(As though hurt)* Why on earth do you ask me questions if every time I answer you you say it isn't true?

MISS GIDDENS. Because you are not answering me! Why don't you tell me the truth!

MILES. I do. But you pay no attention to it. *(Smiling)* Would you like it if I started asking *you* questions?

MISS GIDDENS. I'd answer them—

MILES. *(With terrible directness)* Why, then, aren't we with Mrs. Grose and Flora?

MISS GIDDENS. Because— *(Almost crying)* Ah, Miles, you won't come out with it yourself— How, then, can I?

MILES. *(With delight)* You see? You won't answer my question!

MISS GIDDENS. *(Pleading—no longer trying to control her tears—her tenderness)* Miles, I'm not a cruel person— However unfair I may seem to you—I am not cruel. Sometimes I am foolish— I make mistakes, and, at the moment, I am very tired. But I am not cruel. I was taught to love people and to help them— I was taught to help them even if, sometimes, they didn't want to be helped. Even if, sometimes, it should hurt them. Whatever you may have done, whatever you may have done—I am not against you. I have stayed here to help you— I don't think it's your fault. It *isn't* your fault— Won't you let me help you, won't you?

MILES. *(His whole body rigid. A sneering smile on his face. He stares at her for a full moment)* Why don't you stop pretending?

(They do not move, nor do they take their eyes from each other for a long moment. An absolute silence fastens itself onto the room. Then MISS GIDDENS rises slowly. Her body is as rigid as MILES'—her back as though held by steel. She is stunned, emotionally, but she has not been swayed in her decision. She moves stiffly and with deliberate steps.)

What are you doing?

MISS GIDDENS. *(As she crosses to desk, picks up tray*

of food and crosses to table Right Center) You must be hungry— You—had—no—tea. I kept something for you. Sit down.

MILES. I'm not hungry.

MISS GIDDENS. Sit down.

MILES. *(Sitting down at table)* I've never eaten in here. It isn't a dining-room. What would Mrs. Grose think? *(As* MISS GIDDENS *goes to love-seat)* I'll get crumbs on the carpet— *(As* MISS GIDDENS *pays no attention to him)* Is Flora really ill?

MISS GIDDENS. *(Not looking at him)* She might have become so had she remained.

MILES. *Why* did Mrs. Grose lock her in her room today?

MISS GIDDENS. *(Looking at him as he apparently concentrates on eating)* Don't you know?

MILES. I can guess.

MISS GIDDENS. What?

MILES. *(Slight smile)* She had a fever.

MISS GIDDENS. *(Looking down at her embroidery)* She—did not have a fever. You know that.

(As MISS GIDDENS *continues to sew, the* FIGURE OF QUINT *appears at the window, outlined against the darkness of the garden, his eyes on* MILES' *back. A high VIBRATION is heard, rising as* MILES *stiffens in his chair, fully aware of* QUINT. *He begins to turn his head slowly. As he begins to turn his head,* MISS GIDDENS *raises hers to look at him. She is not aware of* QUINT. MILES *realizes this. With a sudden sweep of his hand he knocks his plate onto the floor. As the plate hits the floor, the VIBRATION stops.* QUINT *disappears from window.)*

MISS GIDDENS. Why did you do that!

MILES. *(Visibly trembling)* Because—because I wanted to. Now—I've made you angry.

MISS GIDDENS. I'm not angry, Miles.

MILES. *(His face strangely drawn)* Yes. You are. You're angry. We're alone and there isn't anyone to talk to and you're angry.

MISS GIDDENS. *(She kneels to pick up tray)* If I am—you've given me reason to be.

(LIGHT #4. Stage area dim.)

MILES. *(Tight-lipped. After a moment)* Weren't your brothers ever naughty?

MISS GIDDENS. Sometimes they were—when they were young.

MILES. *(Tight-lipped)* And now? Are they wicked in a grown-up way?

MISS GIDDENS. I don't know.

MILES. *(His voice dying away—almost peevishly)* I—I wish I could go away—

MISS GIDDENS. *(After a long moment)* To another school—?

MILES. I don't think I should suit *any* school—

MISS GIDDENS. Why do you say that—?

MILES. *(Looking away from her)* Do you think I would?

(The light of the candles barely light MISS GIDDENS *and* MILES.*)*

MISS GIDDENS. I don't see any reason why you wouldn't— *(Pause)* You're like any boy—

MILES. *(Almost a whisper)* Am I? It would be easier, wouldn't it, if we were all alike? There would be no need for these conversations, and you wouldn't be upset and I—I'd be left alone. It's odd, though, but I don't think I'd like it much, and yet I am alone, even now, quite alone.

MISS GIDDENS. Miles!

MILES. *(Does not look at her)* And everything you do makes it worse. Because you don't think I'm like any boy, and you're so certain. *(Turning his head to look at her, slowly)* But *you* may be wrong, you know. *(Slow smile)* And if you are—what on earth shall *you* do? *(As* MISS GIDDENS *continues to look at him)* Is that why you're afraid? *(Softly but with terrible directness)* You *are* afraid, you know— *(Looking at her. Then a sudden burst—and a strange temper)* Why is it so bad—my throwing things on the floor! Why! Other people can do—

MISS GIDDENS. But there's so much more—isn't there!

MILES. *(Looking down quickly—fumbling with his napkin—taking his time. Then in a small, careful voice:)* Is there—? *(Softly)* Other kinds of—naughtiness—? —or what?

MISS GIDDENS. The real reason why you were out in the garden when you were supposed to be in bed!

MILES. *(Quickly—trying to force a smile)* I *told* you it was to show you that I—

MISS GIDDENS. And you took a letter from the desk.

MILES. *(Looking from one spot on the floor to another. Finally staring down at his feet)* Yes. I took it.

(A long moment passes.)

MISS GIDDENS. *(A sharp whisper that has the quality of a scream)* Why did you take it!

MILES. *(Looking down)* To see what you said about me—

MISS GIDDENS. You opened the letter?

MILES. I opened it—

MISS GIDDENS. *(With a tremendous effort)* And— what did you find—?

MILES. You said you were leaving—you said you had to leave— *(Slowly looking up at her. He speaks the words with a careful directness—straight at her)* You said: "Dear Sir, I think that I am ill—"

(Neither moves for a long moment. MILES never takes his eyes off MISS GIDDENS.)

MISS GIDDENS. *(Staring at him—her voice is low and unemotional)* What did you do with the letter—

MILES. I burnt it—

MISS GIDDENS. Did you take other things —Is that what you did at school—

MILES. Did I steal—?

MISS GIDDENS. Was it for *that* that you won't be allowed to go back—?

MILES. *(He waits—as she does not answer)* No. I didn't steal.

MISS GIDDENS. Then—Miles. What *did* you do—

(A low VIBRATION, beginning as an almost inaudible hum, fills the pause—ceasing with MILES' next words.)

MILES. *(Looking, as though in vague pain, all around the room—drawing his breath with difficulty)* I—well—I said things—

MISS GIDDENS. To whom did you say them—

MILES. *(He gives a sick little headshake)* I don't remember their names—

MISS GIDDENS. Were there so many—?

MILES. No—only a few— *(A sickly shame)* Those I liked—

MISS GIDDENS. And they—repeated them—

MILES. To—those they liked. The Masters heard— I didn't know they'd tell.

MISS GIDDENS. The Masters never told— That's why I ask you—

MILES. *(In a low voice)* I suppose they were too bad—the things I said—to write home—

MISS GIDDENS. Miles—

MILES. *(Almost a whisper as he looks down at his feet)* Yes—?

MISS GIDDENS. Where did you first hear these things—?

(Again the VIBRATION is heard. MILES and MISS GIDDENS seem to freeze on MISS GIDDENS' last question.)

MILES. Why—I—I made them up—
MISS GIDDENS. Miles!

(An answering THROB, deep and vibrating, is heard.)

MILES. *(Whisper)* Yes—?
MISS GIDDENS. Who told you to say them? !
MILES. I made them up —I just told you that— *(Edging away from table)* They came into my head— *(He moves to Right and then down, with small pauses and a seemingly casual manner)* I would like to go to bed now. I am tired— May I?
MISS GIDDENS. What were they? ! These things you said—? !
MILES. *(At spinet. Looking down at keys—a strange smile on his face)* You wouldn't like them.
MISS GIDDENS. What were they, Miles—? !
MILES. *(Not turning—still smiling)* You know so much—can't you guess, then?
MISS GIDDENS. Shall I tell you who it was that said them?
MILES. *(Looking at her—quickly)* It was a boy—a boy at school—that's all— I won't say them again— I promise—
MISS GIDDENS. Shall I tell you his name? !
MILES. *(Moving towards stairs, down— Looking at the floor at he walks slowly)* What does it matter? It wasn't anything—
MISS GIDDENS. It wasn't a boy at school—!
MILES. *(Looking at her—sharply, going up stairs)* You can't get away with this, you know! I know why you're doing this!
MISS GIDDENS. What did *he* say to you when you went walking by the pond?
MILES. *(Desperately)* This afternoon? Why, no one was there— Who would be there?
MISS GIDDENS. Not this afternoon!
MILES. When then? Yesterday?

MISS GIDDENS. *(Strongly) Not* yesterday. Before I came here—to live in this house.

(Powerful VIBRATION, sharp, ringing.)

MILES. I was at school!

MISS GIDDENS. And before that? !

(Stronger, sharper VIBRATION.)

MILES. *(His head thrust out towards her)* I know why you're asking me all these questions! You're afraid! That's why!

MISS GIDDENS. *(Cutting in sharply)* And not only the things you said—things you've done!—and what you *might* do—!

MILES. *(Ugly)* O, yes, I *might!* You're afraid— that's why you try to make me admit something— *(Swiftly looking at the window, then at* MISS GID- DENS, *then back to windows, then again at* MISS GID- DENS.)*

MISS GIDDENS. Miles!

MILES. You're in it and you won't stop at anything, will you?

MISS GIDDENS. Miles! I want to help you! Let me help you!

MILES. You keep saying that! But there's nothing you can do, is there? ! Because I know Flora isn't ill— You frightened her because you didn't know what else to do!

MISS GIDDENS. *(Moving towards him)* Miles!

MILES. *(Stepping backwards to staircase)* But *I'm* not a baby! What *are* you going to do! What will you say to my uncle! He'll laugh at you! *(The VIBRA- TION grows all the while: strange tonalities pass above it. A desperation grows in* MILES) I'll tell him! I'll tell him what you're like! He'll believe me! He'll see what you are! Flora will tell him! *I'll* tell him! I'll tell him that you're vile— He won't believe what *you* say! Be- cause you're dirty! Dirty! Dirty!

MISS GIDDENS. You've never stopped seeing him, have you, Miles!

MILES. Don't ask me, Miss Giddens.

MISS GIDDENS. You still want to be with him, don't you, Miles?

MILES. *(Before he can stop himself—a terrible scream)* He's dead!

(As MILES *screams, the figure of* QUINT *appears at the window—standing there, against the darkness of the garden. All the musical VIBRATIONS stop. But a low THUMPING is heard—a sound as that of a heart—low and in a broken rhythm.)*

MISS GIDDENS. *(Now with a desperate pleading)* Who, Miles! His *name!* Give me his name!

MILES. He's dead. He's dead.

(MUSIC Q. Volume 10.)

MISS GIDDENS. Give me his name.

MILES. He'll hurt me. Stop it, Miss Giddens.

MISS GIDDENS. Reject him, for he is here, now, at the window.

MILES. Miss Giddens, you don't know, you don't know.

MISS GIDDENS. Reject him or he'll destroy you. I'm here to help you.

MILES. *(Clinging to her desperately)* You can't. Don't you see? You can't. You don't understand. He'll hurt me. You can't help.

MISS GIDDENS. You will be free. Confess. His name.

MILES. *(Breaking away—then—with a tremendous directness)* Quint! Peter Quint!

MISS GIDDENS. Now. Miles, now.

(For a moment there is almost absolute silence—the only sound is the now loud THUMPING, as of a heart quickening its beat. MUSIC Volume 20. For a second MILES *is still at landing, then, with a tremendous shudder, he forces himself to turn to the window.)*

MILES. *(Facing the window—his arms flung before him. A scream)* Leave me—! Leave me—! *(LIGHT #8. Back lights out. As he screams,* QUINT'S *arms rise before him as though to touch* MILES *across the distance.* MILES' *body begins to crumple. He half-turns back to* MISS GIDDENS. *MUSIC Volume 16. His voice comes thinly and piteously)* Miss Giddens—Miss Gidde— *(He spins as though to escape something. He tries to cry out again—but he falls to the ground.)*
(MUSIC out.)

(The SOUND of a heart stops. QUINT *slowly disappears into the darkness of the garden.)*

(WARN Curtain.)
MISS GIDDENS. *(Moving as though suddenly released—swiftly she goes to* MILES *and kneels beside him, taking him in her arms as if cradling him)* He is gone—he is gone, Miles, dear Miles—and we're alone and nothing can hurt you anymore—nothing can hurt you —I am here and he—he has gone— He can never return. He has lost you and you are free— *(A soft, gentle MUSIC is heard—almost a lullaby.)* Nothing can hurt you anymore—nothing can hurt you. There is only good in you now— Miles, dear Miles— *(She strains him to her)* You see? You are safe—you are safe and I am here with you—to hold you—to help you—to love you— *(Her words are a soft, weeping hysteria)* You see—? I have always wanted to help you—never to hurt you— It was almost too late, Miles, dear Miles—but you've won— You won back goodness and kindness— You are free— *(On these last words she looks down at* MILES.*)*

(Slowly, her arms release his body, and absolute horror marks her face. As MILES' *body falls back, a thin, shrieking SOUND, a musical sound—but dissonant and piercing, is heard. A sudden WIND comes from the garden. The silk curtains at the*

window blow into the room. Dried leaves swirl across the threshold of the window. Even the moonlight, cold and grey, seems to enter and surround MISS GIDDENS *as she kneels beside* MILES' *body.)*

MISS GIDDENS. (MISS GIDDENS' *voice comes sobbingly)*—you are free—you're free. You're free—

(Then her sobs distort her words and cover them and hide them as—)

SLOW CURTAIN

Samuel French, Inc. can supply a Sound Effect Cassette or Reel to Reel Tape for $32.50. Add $3.00 for UPS shipment.

THE INNOCENTS

HAND PROPERTY PLOT

Oil lamp—battery
Oil lamp—electric
One stick brass candle holder
Two stick silver Georgian candelabra
Accessories for letter writing (inkwell, paper, quill)
Dried leaves
Two small travelling bags
Tea tray and accessories for tea
Books
Two letters
Small photograph
Tapers and matches
Hand embroidery and frame
Box of pencils
Pin cushion
Slate pencils and slates
Handkerchief
Pack of cards
Plate of cakes
Two hymnals
Dead beetle
Pictures to be cut out
Scissors
Small tea tray—glass of milk, bread and butter
Napkin
Paper knife
Two dusters
Work basket—sewing things
Thunder machine
Clock chime
Flower basket

THE INNOCENTS

PROPERTY PLOT

ACT ONE, Scene I

Letters and photograph in desk drawer
All French windows shut
Silk curtains open
Drapes open
Book on desk
Writing paper on desk
Inkwell on desk
Quill on desk
Battery oil lamp on desk
Matches on desk
Leaves under love-seat
Ottoman fringe unhooked
Spinet top open
Small table Right of love-seat
Love-seat
Stool
Desk
Chair behind desk
Ottoman
Armchair
Spinet
Large cabinet
Four rugs
Matches and ash tray on spinet
Paper knife on desk

Ready off Right:
    Tea tray and accessories
    Taper
    Books
    Slates
    Slate pencils
    Flower basket
    Dressing-up clothes
    Candelabra
Ready off Left:
    Travelling bag
    Sewing things and basket
    Dusters

ACT ONE, Scene II

All French windows shut
Silk curtains drawn shut
Drapes drawn one-third
Spinet stool shift under spinet
Strike tea table—Right of sofa
Strike jacket and bonnet

ACT ONE, Scene III

All French windows open
Silk curtains open
Drapes open
Letters on desk—one with photo
Open spinet top
Replace battery lamp with electric—table Left

ACT ONE, Scene IV

Center French window open—other two shut
Silk curtains drawn one-third
Drapes open
Strike letters
Strike flower basket

ACT TWO, Scene III

Center French window open—other two shut
Silk curtains drawn shut
Drapes open
Tea tray, glass of milk, sandwich on desk
Embroidery frame on sofa
Miles' coat and travelling bag ready Left
Strike shawl
Strike hat and gloves
Table to side of armchair, Right Center
Desk chair shifted into desk

ACT ONE, Scene V .

All French windows shut
Silk curtains open
Drapes open
Embroidery on ottoman
Spinet stool out from under spinet
Strike hat and gloves

ACT TWO, Scene I

All French windows shut
Silk curtains one-half drawn
Drapes drawn shut
Replace electric lamp with battery lamp
Playing cards ready Right
Cut out pictures and scissors in cabinet
Cake and plate ready Right
Candlestick on piano
Spinet stool shift under spinet
Platform door to mark
Strike taper
Strike pin cushion
Strike slates and pencils
Strike embroidery
Close spinet top

ACT TWO, Scene II

Center French window open—other two shut
Silk curtains open
Drapes drawn one-third
Two hymnals ready Left
Dead beetle on floor Left of ottoman
Strike playing cards
Strike cake plate
Shawl ready Right
Blow out candle on spinet
Replace battery lamp with electric lamp—Right side
    of table

THE INNOCENTS

COSTUME PLOT

ACT ONE, Scene I

MISS GIDDENS: Brown dress, jacket, brown bonnet, brown gloves

MRS. GROSE: Brown dress, black apron, lace cap, black mitts, silver chain, black shoes, wig, petticoat, 2 pair black hose

FLORA: White dress, black slippers, 2 pair white hose, 2 panties

ACT ONE, Scene II

MISS GIDDENS: Same, without jacket and accessories

MRS. GROSE: Blue dress, black apron, lace cap, lace mitts

FLORA: Nightgown, bed slippers

ACT ONE, Scene III

MISS GIDDENS: Tan check dress

MRS. GROSE: Same

FLORA: Blue dress, black slippers

ACT ONE, Scene IV

MISS GIDDENS: Same. Brown bonnet, gloves

MRS. GROSE: Same

FLORA: Same. Faun coat, gloves and straw hat

MILES: Gray topcoat, black cap, black pumps, blue coat, gray pants, 2 white shirts, 2 black ties

ACT ONE, Scene V

Miss Giddens: Same, without gloves and bonnet
Mrs. Grose: Same
Flora: Same, without coat, hat and gloves
Miles: Same, without topcoat and cap

ACT TWO, Scene I

Miss Giddens: Purple dress
Mrs. Grose: Brown dress, lace cap, lace mitts
Flora: Nightgown, bed slippers
Miles: Nightgown, bed slippers

ACT TWO, Scene II

Miss Giddens: Same
Mrs. Grose: Brown dress, check cape, black bonnet
Flora: White dress, faunt coat and bonnet, gloves, button shoes

ACT TWO, Scene III

Miss Giddens: Same, with black shawl
Mrs. Grose: Same
Miles: Same

Quint: 3 piece gray suit, 2 gray shirts, 1 black bow, 1 pair gray gloves
Miss Jessel: 1 black dress, 1 black hat and veil, 1 pair black gloves
Playclothes:
    Miles: Yellow sash and towel turban
    Flora: Drape and pin cushion with pins

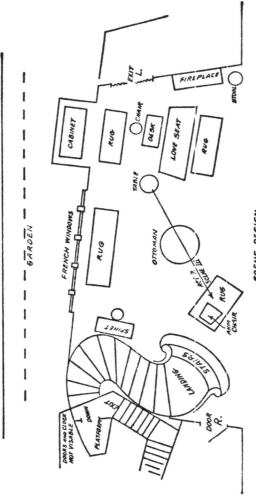

SCENE DESIGN
"THE INNOCENTS"

CPSIA information can be obtained at www.ICGtesting.com
Printed in the USA
LVOW04s1014010914

401754LV00003B/126/P